C'NC INDIAN WAR

BORDER CLASH
OCTOBER–NOVEMBER 1962

GERRY VAN TONDER

Pen & Sword

81 001 70 3

First published in Great Britain in 2018 by
PEN AND SWORD MILITARY
an imprint of
Pen and Sword Books Ltd
47 Church Street
Barnsley
South Yorkshire S70 2AS

ISBN 978 1 526728 37 1

Typeset by Aura Technology and Software Services, India
Maps, drawings and militaria in the colour section by Colonel Dudley Wall
Printed and bound by CPI Group (UK) Ltd, Croydon CR0 4YY

Pen & Sword Books Ltd incorporates the imprints of Pen & Sword
Archaeology, Atlas, Aviation, Battleground, Discovery, Family History, History, Maritime, Military,
Naval, Politics, Railways, Select, Social History, Transport, True Crime, Claymore Press, Frontline
Books, Leo Cooper, Praetorian Press, Remember When, Seaforth Publishing and Wharncliffe.

For a complete list of Pen and Sword titles please contact
Pen and Sword Books Limited
47 Church Street, Barnsley, South Yorkshire, S70 2AS, England
email: enquiries@pen-and-sword.co.uk
website: www.pen-and-sword.co.uk

CONTENTS

TIMELINE

1846
Britain recognizes the sovereignty of Gulab Singh Dogra as maharajah of Jammu and Kashmir.
The Treaty of Amritsar is signed.

1847
British commissioners complete a mapped boundary in the direction of Tibet, noting that certain swathes of uninhabited *terra incognita* could not be defined.

1849
Britain annexes the Punjab.

1865
Surveyor W. H. Johnson demarcates the border line between the Pangong Lake and the Karakorum Pass, incorporating the region of Aksai Chin.

1866
Independent Kashgaria is formed under Muslim Yaqub Beg as Chinese rule is overthrown.

1877
Kashgaria is reconquered by the Chinese General Zuo Zongtang during the Qing reconquest of Xinjiang.

1892
China erects a boundary marker in the Karakorum Pass, effectively claiming ownership of the 'no-man's land' beyond the pass.

1893
The Durand Line is agreed to, delineating the mountainous border between tribal Afghanistan and British India.

1896
British and Chinese authorities both claim territorial ownership of the Aksai Chin.

1899

China ignores British boundary alignment proposals: the Macartney–MacDonald Line, which would establish Aksai Chin as part of Tibet and not Xinjiang.

1907

Britain negotiates with Russia a convention of mutual non-interference in the affairs of Tibet.

1914

The Simla Convention between Britain, China and Tibet allows for the formation of 'Inner' and 'Outer' Tibet, the latter as an autonomous Chinese territory. Henry McMahon heads the British delegation.
Britain and Tibet agree to an Assam–Tibet boundary: the McMahon Line.
China does not accept this demarcation.

1937

Official Survey of India charts start to show the McMahon Line as India's northeast boundary. The Tawang Tract is shown as part of Tibet.

1947

India is granted its independence from Britain.
Tibet formally asks India to return the region from Ladakh to Assam.

1949

Tibet expels the Chinese mission from the capital, Lhasa, and seeks military aid from India.
The Communist People's Republic of China is formed.

1950

China declares its sovereignty over Tibet.

1951

Chinese Premier Zhou Enlai calls on India for a stabilization of the Tibetan boundary.

1954

An agreement on 'Trade and Intercourse' between the Tibet Region of China and India is signed in Beijing.

1956

Chinese frontier guards spearhead construction of a 750-mile-long road across Aksai Chin, including 112 miles over territory claimed by India.

Zhou Enlai, during talks in New Delhi, raises the boundary issue of the McMahon Line.

1958

India formally lays claim to Aksai Chin, while expressing 'surprise and regret' at China's construction of a road across its territory.

1959

Indian Prime Minister Jawaharlal Nehru, reacting to a request from Zhou, states that the McMahon Line boundary is not open to negotiation.

The Tibetan Uprising sees the Dalai Lama and his government in support of the anti-Chinese rebels. He flees to India.

25 August: First exchange of fire on the McMahon Line.

8 September: Zhou reasserts Peking's ownership between the McMahon Line and the foothills, and demands the withdrawal of 'trespassing' Indian forces and administrative personnel from Chinese territory.

21 October: Nine Indian troops killed and seven taken prisoner after a brief contact with elements of the People's Liberation Army (PLA) at the Kongka Pass.

1960

19 April: Following a request from Nehru, Zhou heads a large Chinese delegation to New Delhi for talks on the border dispute.

The Chinese offer concessions in the eastern sector in exchange for similar gestures of goodwill from the Indians in the western sector.

The summit is a failure.

1961

India continues with the full implementation of its 'Forward Policy' in the disputed border areas, deploying armed forces on active patrolling and establishing outposts. The PLA emulates this military activity.

1962

Indian forces establish twenty-four new posts along the McMahon Line.

May: The Indian XXXIII Corps moves west of the Khinzemane area, establishing a post—Dhola—at Che Dong, four miles north of the India–China–Bhutan trijunction.

Operation Leghorn is formulated to push the PLA back over the Thag La Ridge at Dhola.

10 October: A battalion of PLA attacks Indian positions, signalling the start of the conflict.

21 November: China declares a ceasefire along the entire border with India.

1 December: The PLA is withdrawn twenty miles from the disputed frontier.

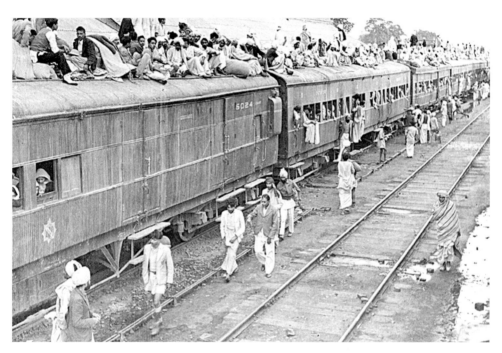

Apart from the vast population upheavals, the partition of India in 1947 was defined by ill-advised border delineations on the northwestern and northeastern frontiers, the ramifications of which would stretch into the future for many generations. (Photo Government of India)

INTRODUCTION

In mid-1962, a flare-up in the Sino-Indian border dispute was sparked off by recent Indian forward movements into the disputed border area of Ladakh. Indian troops were reported to have occupied one outpost and were under orders to secure a larger one several miles farther out. Beijing strongly denunciated the Indian military moves, demanding an immediate withdrawal and stating that it would forcefully defend the positions it controlled. Indian premier Jawaharlal Nehru informed parliament that India would continue to protect the integrity of the Himalayan border area, and was preparing for the contingency of war with China to achieve this.

The preservation of Indian territorial and political interests in the Himalayas had long been a fundamental aspect of Nehru's policy of Indian sovereignty. As a loyal adherent to the passive teachings of Mahatma Gandhi, Nehru had originally sought cordial relations with Beijing, basing his policy on *Panch Shila* or the Five Principles of Peaceful Coexistence. However, from 1954, there had been several Chinese incursions into Indian-claimed territory. In 1959, Beijing brutally quashed the Tibetan revolt, followed thereafter by increased efforts to bring the border states of Bhutan, Sikkim and Nepal within its sphere of influence.

Up until 1960, New Delhi had a tacit understanding that the mountainous northern border status quo would be maintained, but further Chinese encroachments in 1961 exacerbated what had essentially been a brittle situation. Now, Nehru and well-informed Indians started nurturing the belief that their interests could not be best served without a demonstrable determination to resort to force in their defence.

Realistically, India most likely did not believe that it could make good its claims to all the territory in Ladakh, asserting that this was a real-estate legacy inherited from the British at independence. In fact, the Aksai Chin plateau area in eastern Ladakh was of far greater use and accessibility to China than to India, China having, in 1957, constructed a road across the disputed region connecting Tibet and Xinjiang. Of prime concern to Nehru, therefore, was the establishment of a show of military strength and a pattern of occupation designed to prevent further Chinese expansion to therefore leave New Delhi in a favourable negotiating position for a settlement of a whole tranche of border issues. This meant that efforts would have to be made to push back Chinese incursions which appeared to expand the limits of the disputed area.

Nehru stressed India's imperative to actively maintain the nation's claims to any of the disputed border areas, warning that a failure to do so would dangerously

FIERCE FIGHTING IN TIBET

Dalai Lama Reaches the Assam Plains
Fierce fighting has broken out between Tibetan rebels and Chinese troops in the Chamdo area of East Tibet, *The Times of India* said yesterday.

"Chamdo is like an island protected by a Chinese garrison," said the paper quoting reliable sources from Gangtok, Sikkim. It was also reported from Gangtok that the Chinese are moving into Western Tibet in an all-out attempt to block escape-route passes leading to Nepal and Kashmir. Other reports said that twin-engined bombers are arriving at an airport 150 miles north of Lhasa and that planes resembling Soviet MiG 15s are flying in waves to reconnoitre all possible escape routes. The military airport at Lhasa, damaged by Tibetan rebels, has been repaired and is strongly guarded by contingents of the Chinese army, reports said.

Khamba tribesmen were said to be running desperately short of supplies and ammunition.

To Put it Down
The Times of India quoted a high Chinese official in the border town of Kalimpong as saying that his Government had decided to put down the Tibetan rebellion once and for all. The Dalai Lama yesterday completed the most perilous stretch of his pony trek toward the Assam plains crossing the 14,500 ft. Se Las pass and descending into Sang Dzong, a Buddhist village 25 miles from Tawang monastery where he had been resting. Peking Radio reported yesterday that the Panchen Lama, installed by the Chinese in place of the Dalai Lama, has left Lhasa for Peking. He will attend the Chinese National Congress on April 17. Taipeh newspapers claimed yesterday that 200,000 tribesmen are fighting the Chinese Communists in the border area of Szechwan and Sikang provinces in China's far west.

Birmingham Daily Post, Friday, 10 April 1959

compromise the country's security by calling into question the validity of the entire border demarcation inherited from their former colonial masters. Public awareness and opinion would be key to any future action. Nehru's reputation as India's founding premier was also at stake, and with the electorate watching on, the long-term military build-up for the defence of the northern border commenced.

For New Delhi, the timing of an escalation in border tensions was unusually for-tuitous in terms of asserting its territorial claims as the People's Republic of China (PRC) was experiencing significant internal difficulties. Not only were Beijing's rela-tions with the Soviet Union strained, but Moscow had refused to support Beijing in their border dispute with India; in fact, Moscow was willing to provide non-aligned India with military hardware. Added to this, Nehru was confident that the West could be relied on to endorse Indian actions, and, should it become necessary, to pro-vide direct support.

The dispute with India was of equal importance to the PRC, who similarly main-tained that India's claims in the Himalayas were based on unilateral treaties forced upon an unwilling China in the days of the British Raj. For Beijing, control of the Aksai Chin was of fundamental importance to maintain a secure position in western Tibet. To back down in the face of Indian military determination would jeopardize this strategic objective and be detrimental to its standing as an independent communist state.

The Tibetan uprising, which started in Lhasa in March 1959, followed by sporadic border clashes with India, did much to tarnish the image that Beijing was trying to nurture as a powerful but essentially benevolent leader in Asia. For the PRC, there-fore, damage limitation was important, but not at the expense of negating its strategic interests. Beijing demonstrated significant levels of good-neighbourly cordiality in reaching border agreements with Burma in 1960 and Nepal in 1961, while continuing to seek negotiations with India. India, however, remained obstinately uncompromis-ing in its responses to overtures from Beijing, leaving the Chinese in a seemingly no-win position with its diplomatic tactics.

In a high-stakes game of posturing, Indian activity in Ladakh also hardened the PRC's determination to defend its position. In a missive to New Delhi, dated 30 April 1962, Beijing stated that its troops had been ordered to resume border patrols in the Ladakh area, something it had claimed it had ceased two years ago. It was unequiv-ocal in its threat to resume patrolling along the entire shared frontier. On 3 May, the PRC and Pakistan jointly announced their agreement to negotiate a provisional delimitation of the frontier between Xinjiang and Pakistan, an undertaking that included Pakistani-occupied Kashmir, a move guaranteed to further exacerbate Sino-Indian as well as Indo-Pakistani relations.

Accessibility to the Sino-Indian border region, highly problematic in the hostile, mountainous wilderness of the Himalayas, made extensive or sustained military operations extremely difficult for both antagonists. Throughout the year, particularly in winter, the maintenance of even small military outposts, many at an elevation of over 16,000 feet, was a logistical nightmare for both sides. Albeit that the PRC had significantly longer supply lines, it did generally enjoy easier ground access to the disputed area than did India. In more recent years, the Chinese had also improved their propensity for redeploying troops from one place to another by developing a route parallel to much of the border for use by military transport. However, border approaches from the Indian side, over much rougher terrain, were for the most part restricted to rudimentary trails that met the border at right angles. Especially in the Aksai Chin, Indian supplies had to navigate several high passes. As a consequence, both sides depended heavily on pack animals for supply. The Indians also used air-drop delivery where and when possible.

At the time, major Indian troop concentrations along the border were found in three widely separated areas: the Ladakh region of Kashmir, Sikkim and the North East Frontier Agency, or NEFA. India had thirteen infantry brigades in Kashmir, but eleven were deployed westward to defend and police the ceasefire line with Pakistan.

Indian forces in Ladakh, operating in company-sized units or less, were supplied as far as Leh via an overland route which was passable most of the year, but aircraft and pack animals were required to supplement motor transport. The sole, understrength infantry division and several local rifle battalions located in NEFA had to be supplied in the same manner. However, India's road infrastructure was more capable of supporting the reinforced brigade group in Sikkim.

Potala Palace, Lhasa, former residence of the Dalai Lama. (Photo Luca Galuzzi)

There were about 110,000 Chinese People's Liberation Army (PLA) troops in Tibet, around twice the number deployed there before the 1959 uprising. Of this number, it was estimated at the time that around 40,000 troops were stationed in eastern Tibet, 48,000 in and around the Tibetan capital Lhasa and about 20,000 along the border with Nepal. In addition, there were also an estimated 34,000 troops in Xinjiang Province, mostly in the north and east. Indian intelligence estimated a presence of 2,800 in the Aksai Chin area of Ladakh, supported by a further 7,000 reserves within 180 miles.

The PLA had two main access roads at their disposal: Yarkand–Gartok and Galmo–Lhasa. The latter was the main supply route for the military units in Tibet. The Chinese were also constructing east–west roads within Tibet and connecting roads to Nepal.

Domestic economic instability curtailed the PRC's resupply and reinforcement capabilities in the Indian border area, with the maintenance of sustainable troop levels in Tibet severely stretching its logistic capabilities. Beijing was therefore hamstrung in its abilities to meaningfully augment troop deployment in Tibet to any sizeable extent: it had neither the motor transport nor the fuel and oil. A lack of developed air facilities in the area and the extreme length of Chinese supply lines limited Beijing's air capability, particularly for combat operations.

Despite the important national interests and pride involved that vigorously injected both India and China with patriotic fervour, there were major factors that caused both sides to exercise caution lest the tempo of their quarrel escalated out of control.

The Indians were not confident that they had the resources to cope with the vast Chinese military power should significant escalation take place. On the other hand, the Chinese were fully aware that their dispute with India had generated widespread criticism within the communist bloc, making them reluctant to heighten the conflict, especially in Ladakh where they had already occupied the contested territory. Added to this, the very nature of the theatre involved meant that the logistical support of even relatively small military operations would place unsustainable burdens on respective national economies already under considerable strain. Finally, any intensification of the border dispute would, in all likelihood, restrict the ability of both the PRC and India to deal with other national issues of more pressing importance.

However, further clashes became inevitable, particularly in the Aksai Chin area. Rhetoric and frontier activities had committed both sides to the point where neither was prepared to face the humiliation of backing off. India ordered 1,800 additional troops into the Ladakh area, compelling Beijing to respond in like manner. Inherent in such tit-for-tat tactics came the risk of clashes occurring elsewhere along the common border.

BRITAIN 'CANNOT STOP' ORDER FOR RUSSIA—NEHRU

Mr. Nehru today told the Indian Parliament that Britain could not stop India buying Russian Mig supersonic jet lighters, and added: "There is no question of consulting Britain about our defence.

"It has been our practice in the past to buy our defence equipment largely from the United Kingdom, partly from the United States, and partly from France and other countries."

That did not mean that "they can come in the way" of India buying Migs. Mr. Nehru said nobody, to his knowledge, had so far stated that India had no right to buy defence equipment from whatever source she liked.

Sandys' Statement
Britain, naturally, wanted India to continue to buy British. "They are sellers, and they want to sell their goods, which no doubt they want to sell at a profit."

A Communist member had drawn the Prime Minister's attention to a statement by the Commonwealth Relations Secretary, Mr. Sandys, that he was satisfied India would consult with Britain before taking a final step on the aircraft issue. The member asked whether it was practice for India to consult Britain about India's defence equipment purchases. The Communist leader, Mr. Phupesh Gupta, asked why Britain had offered fighters to India only after the Soviet Union had offered to sell India Migs.

Mr. Nehru said: "I do not know how the member got the impression that the Soviet Government made any offer to us. I know of no such offer."

China Problem
Mr. Nehru said an Indian Air Force team which visited the Soviet Union about three months ago to buy an engine for India's own Hindustan HF-24 supersonic jet fighter, became interested in Migs. Asked if India would be free to use Migs against China, Mr. Nehru said once aircraft were bought or produced in India, they became Indian property and India would use them wherever the need arose.

Pressed for further information, the Prime Minister replied angrily: "I cannot go on discussing a matter which should not be discussed."

Coventry Evening Telegraph, Wednesday, 20 June 1962

In Washington, American intelligence suggested that patrol actions and relatively small-scale encounters—"possibly accompanied by occasional minor air clashes"—rather than pitched battles would characterize any resort to arms. Concern, however, was expressed that, as increasing numbers of opposing troops come into contact with each other, the chances of miscalculation or overzealous action by local commanders in the field would grow. Although the odds were strongly against a major escalation of the military conflict spreading beyond the Himalayan theatre, the political and psychological stakes involved in even relatively small-scale actions could progressively spiral in intensity, making it increasingly difficult for either side to back down.

Politically, it was therefore in the interests of both India and the PRC to increase their efforts to expand their regional influence with the Himalayan border states. New Delhi's dominance was already established in Sikkim, but its position in Bhutan was less so. In spite of this, however, the PRC would have to tread softly lest its efforts caused Bhutan to increase its reliance on India as it had after Beijing's ruthless quashing of the Tibetan uprising. Although India also maintained a not insignificant influence in Nepal, its reluctance to curtail the activities of Nepali opposition leaders in India had resulted in King Mahendra Bir Bikram Shah of Nepal seeking closer relations with Beijing. While the Nepalese monarch's imposition of direct rule in his kingdom generated unresolved problems with India, the mountain state remained susceptible to a wide range of overtures from the PRC.

Tibetan monks, 1939.
(Photo Bundesarchiv)

While both New Delhi and Beijing felt an imperative to flex their military muscle, both favoured a resolution without having to resort to all-out confrontation. Negotiations would remain a possibility, especially if a period of relative calm on the border allowed for public opinion in India to become less zealous. The PRC had already indicated that it would forsake its claims to NEFA in exchange for India's recognition of the PRC's territorial claims in Ladakh. Historically, Nehru had refused to entertain any such compromise. Instead, the Indian premier would be prepared to offer the PRC continued use of their road across Aksai Chin in exchange for recognition of Indian sovereignty over the plateau. Barring a total but very unlikely domestic collapse of the communist regime in Beijing, the PRC would not agree to abandon its position on Ladakh. Against this scenario, it was improbable that either of the belligerents would find satisfaction in any form of negotiation.

In the context of the global Cold War, while PLA pressures on India's borders continued unabated, New Delhi would fully abide by its declared policy of non-alignment by seeking military aid on a selective basis from both the East and West. Nehru harboured a theory that the Soviet Union was in a better position to restrain the PRC than the West, so India would initially look more to Moscow than to Washington to combat perceived Chinese expansionism on its borders. The U.S. was better placed to help in keeping Pakistan off India's back, and for increased economic support to make up for local resources diverted to military purposes.

For the Soviet Union, the Sino-Indian border clashes presented a particular dilemma. If it ventured too far in its support of India, it would seriously exacerbate the Sino-Soviet rift, possibly to the point of an open split within the Marxist-Leninist club. However, if it refused India's requests for aid—including MiG-21 fighter aircraft—it would run the risk of alienating the world's leading neutralist power. If this were to happen, it would destroy the influence it had spent hundreds of millions of aid dollars to establish, and weaken Moscow's influence in the entire Afro-Asian non-aligned world. By going public in their efforts to source military hardware from Moscow, New Delhi had effectively placed Moscow in an embarrassing situation.

Historically, the Soviet Union had privately exerted pressure on the PRC to reach an amicable settlement of the border dispute, while simultaneously providing aid to India, including military equipment used by the border forces. Moscow continued in its refusal to publicly take sides in the Sino-Indian dispute, essentially fence-sitting.

Any continuation or intensification of the Sino-Indian border dispute would pose less of a problem for the U.S. than for the Soviet Union, but it would still involve potential difficulties. By mid-1962, the Indian defence budget has already been increased from $561 million to $730 million since the evolution of the dispute in 1959. Further increases would follow. Such rerouting of Indian resources to defence purposes tended to inhibit progress in the development of the young Indian economy, forcing New Delhi to turn more and more to Washington for economic support. More importantly, the U.S. could not allow the Soviet Union to assume the role of principal provider and thus gain substantial advantages on the subcontinent. Conversely, the U.S. could not provide major assistance to India without risking censure from Pakistan and perhaps other regional allies.

While Pakistan would seek to exploit India's problems with the PRC by propaganda, diplomatic efforts and subtle subversive activities in Kashmir, it was unlikely to become directly involved militarily. However, there would be no compromise by either Pakistan or India to the Kashmir question.

The stakes were high, national pride was on the table, but many were the imponderables and unknowns, not just between the two Asian antagonists but also between the world's only two superpowers, themselves engaged in a much more dangerous face-off over the delivery of Soviet missiles to Cuba, a stone's throw away from the American mainland.

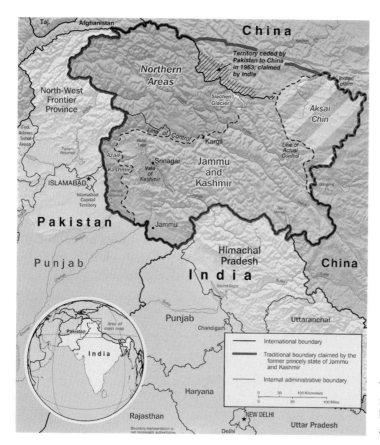

The disputed northwest Indian borders with Pakistan and China. (CIA)

1. DEFENCE OF THE REALM

The Sino-Indian border dispute, unlike most others, owes much to its past. Fundamental factors underlying the dispute can be traced back to post-Second World War independent India and Communist China. Prior to this, nearly a hundred years of competition between imperial Britain and China, and previous centuries that saw military expeditions across the Himalayan mountains as early as 647 AD, contributed to the tensions. Doyens of Indian history date their country's cultural claim to the Himalaya as far back as 1500 BC, the fountainhead of Hindu civilization. The Chinese would have no trouble delving even further back into their dynastical annals for similar supporting evidence.

Historically, the ancient kingdom of Tibet has always been the theatre of Sino-Indian confrontation. As Victorian Britain consolidated its tenure over the Indian subcontinent during the latter half of the nineteenth century, it increasingly began to look at the sprawling and heavily populated nation's northern frontiers. The integrity of the British Raj was dependent on Whitehall instruments of security policies that, over time, had evolved into the absolute importance of Tibet to the northeast and Afghanistan to the northwest as buffers against any threat from Manchurian China and Czarist Russia.

China's rulers had always claimed dominion over Tibet to a lesser or greater extent, depending on the level to which China's regional power waxed and waned. As the power of the Manchu dynasty began to disintegrate toward the end of the nineteenth century, China's role of overlord in Tibet became nominally titular. London was quick to exploit the vacuum, seizing the opportunity to actively pursue a 'forward policy' which ultimately extended India's sphere of influence as far as the religious and administrative Tibetan capital, Lhasa. With the demise of the Manchu regime and the establishment of the Republic of China in 1912, Peking was unable to reassert its control over Tibet.

Britain's determination to secure the Tibetan frontier peaked the following year when London sponsored a tripartite conference at Simla (now Shimla), a mountain resort and the largest city in the northern Indian state of Himachal Pradesh. It is bordered by Jammu and Kashmir to the north, Punjab and Chandigarh on the west, and Tibet to the east. Plenipotentiaries from Britain, China and Tibet met to negotiate an agreement that would define Tibet's political status in relation to China and India. The British hoped to conclude an agreement that would be the culmination of a series of treaties it had already signed with the Himalayan

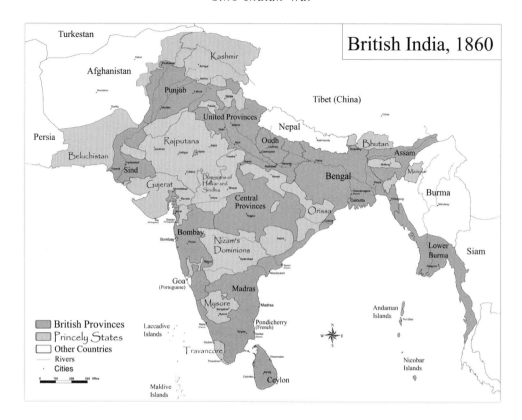

border states such as Sikkim and Burma and, in so doing, establish Britain as the dominant power in the region.

Today, the Simla conference is chiefly remembered for the establishment of the McMahon Line, the boundary drawn on the conference map to delineate the frontier between India and Tibet from Bhutan eastward, to Burma. Named after the British plenipotentiary to Simla, Sir Henry McMahon, who introduced the initiative, the line would follow the crest ridge of the Great Himalayan range as the natural Indo-Tibetan boundary. However, and through either indifference or ignorance, the line was drawn on a small-scale map, giving only a rough and ill-defined indication of the actual border. The Himalayan crest along this northeast sector is broken in a number of places by river gorges and bisecting ranges, and was, as yet, largely *terra incognita*.

However, the proposed division of Tibet into two distinct regions, to be known as Inner and Outer Tibet, proved contentious and divisive. Under such a political delineation, Peking's authority would be limited to those areas of Tibet bordering on China's southwestern provinces, while 'Outer' Tibet, which would include Lhasa and all of western Tibet, would be granted full autonomy status.

Although its plenipotentiary had initialled the draft convention at Simla, signifying acceptance, the Chinese government refused to sign or be party to the treaty. Peking's objections referred to the proposed boundary between Inner and Outer Tibet only. It was apparent at the time that the McMahon Line dividing India and Tibet was not challenged by China.

In July 1914, the British and Tibetan delegates, in the absence of the Chinese member, unilaterally signed the Simla Convention. At Delhi in March that year, Britain and Tibet had already endorsed notes and a map delineating the McMahon Line in greater detail.

With the outbreak of the First World War, the spotlight on the Tibetan issue waned sharply as Britain and her allies were forced to divert their attentions to far more pressing issues, particularly in Europe. Ignoring the absence of a Chinese signature to the Simla Convention, London let it officially be known that it considered the Simla accords to be equally binding on the three governments concerned.

Convention between Great Britain and China over Tibet, 1906.

During the interwar years, the Tibetan issue remained largely dormant. Lhasa enjoyed its state of de facto autonomy, while border security gave New Delhi little cause for concern. With the arrival of the invading Japanese Kwantung Army in Manchuria in September 1931, the Nationalist Chinese government tried to reassert Chinese influence in Tibet in 1933 and 1938, but these advances from Peking were spurned by the Tibetan authorities.

From late 1948, the newly independent India displayed cordial feelings toward the Chinese Communists as they also entered a new phase of national sovereignty. However, this state of good neighbourliness was rudely shattered when 40,000 troops of the Chinese People's Liberation Army crossed the Tibetan border at Chamdo in October 1950. Surrounding the outnumbered Tibetan forces and capturing the town, the PLA ceased hostilities. A message was conveyed to Lhasa inviting representatives of the Dalai Lama to Beijing to negotiate a new Chinese-controlled status for the mountain kingdom.

On 23 May 1951, the seventeen-point 'Agreement of the Central People's Government and the Local Government of Tibet on Measures for the Peaceful Liberation of Tibet' was signed in Beijing, facilitating the Tibetan people to "return to the family of the Motherland the People's Republic of China (PRC)". That October, the Dalai Lama formally acquiesced to Chinese suzerainty in a telegram to Beijing:

> The Tibet Local Government as well as the ecclesiastic and secular people unanimously support this agreement, and under the leadership of Chairman Mao and the Central People's Government, will actively support the People's Liberation Army in Tibet to consolidate national defence, drive out imperialist influences from Tibet and safeguard the unification of the territory and the sovereignty of the Motherland.

Seemingly overnight, the territorial integrity of India's Himalayan frontier had again become a major problem, but this time it would no longer be a British colonial issue, but one for fledgling Indian Prime Minister Jawaharlal Nehru. Nehru would come to regard the Chinese 'liberation' of Tibet in 1950/51 as the catalyst of his dispute with Beijing. Against a backdrop of an alarmed legislature, for the first time Nehru invoked the controversial McMahon Line and the Himalayan crest range as "India's magnificent frontier" as the irrefutable, and therefore inalienable, Sino-Indian border.

New Delhi began gradually taking constrained steps in strengthening its armed forces in the frontier regions, Nehru preferring to focus his attention on diplomatic solutions. During 1950/51, he sought guarantees from Beijing that Tibet's autonomy would be respected. By 1952, India had signed new accords with the buffer states of Bhutan, Sikkim and Nepal, aimed primarily at securing these strategic states within its sphere of influence. Further pursuing his desire for a peaceful, diplomatic resolution to the frontier issues with Beijing, Nehru also pressured Beijing for an agreement that would regularize his country's commercial and cultural ties with Tibet.

The much-vaunted Sino-Indian 'Panch Shila' (from Sanskrit *panch*: five, *sheel*: virtues), signed on 29 April 1954, was the desired outcome, in which India recognized China's sovereignty over "the Tibet region of China". Incorporating the so-called Five Principles of Peaceful Coexistence, entreating non-interference in others' internal affairs and respect for each other's territorial unity integrity and sovereignty. In hindsight, perhaps it was naïve of Nehru at the Asian Prime Ministers Conference in Colombo, Ceylon—only days after the signing—to state: "If these principles were recognized in the mutual relations of all countries, then indeed there would hardly be any conflict and certainly no war."

In 1953, Beijing subtly embarked on psychological 'cartographic aggression'. New Chinese maps were periodically produced in the communist state, clearly showing the disputed border areas as territorially falling within China. New Delhi lodged formal protests, but the Chinese defended their actions by saying that they were merely reproducing Nationalist Chinese maps so that any future changes would be based on informed decisions derived from surveys and collaboration with its neighbours.

New Delhi, guided by the fifth of the Panch Shila principles, advocating 'peaceful co-existence', tried to downplay the ominous significance of these territorial differences, albeit that within certain influential Indian political circles there was growing disquiet that a potentially major border dispute was looming.

In late 1957, these concerns grew considerably when New Delhi discovered, to its chagrin, that the Chinese had constructed a road bisecting the northeastern corner of the Indian-claimed region of Ladakh, the Aksai Chin, an inhospitable, barren plateau never included in New Delhi's administration. A clandestine military team deployed in the spring of 1958 to reconnoitre the disputed area was captured by a Chinese patrol in what would be the first major frontier incident. For more than a year, both China and India kept the whole incident under wraps until the autumn of 1959 when armed clashes on the northeast frontier, as well as in Ladakh, dramatically pushed the border dispute into the public domain.

The 1959 clashes, a consequence of Beijing's quashing of the Tibetan revolt during the spring of that year, resulted in a significant escalation in official and public rhetoric and antagonism between China and India. With the Dalai Lama fleeing Lhasa into exile in India in March, the Chinese bolstered their troop strengths in Tibet, occupying the Himalayan border passes in an effort to stem the flow of Tibetan refugees, while guarding against an ingression of war matériel and Tibetan resistance fighters.

"WE WILL DEFEND OUR FRONTIERS"—Mr. Nehru

Parliament Told of Chinese Attacks

Mr. Nehru, the Prime Minister, told Parliament in New Delhi yesterday that India had put the army in control of the entire sprawling 35,000 square-mile North-East Frontier Agency, where the Chinese had committed aggression from Tibet. There had been firing "for a considerable time," he said. An outpost had been almost encircled in the Subansiri area and had run short of ammunition. Subsequently the Indians withdrew from the outpost.

In the tumultuous atmosphere of the House, Mr. Nehru was at first understood to have said that fighting was still continuing, but the official text of his statement available later made it clear that this was not so.

Authoritative sources in New Delhi also said later that 38 members of the Assam Rifles had been forced to abandon Longju outpost in the Subansiri area and were making their way to the next outpost, Limeking, 20 miles to the South. These sources said Chinese troops were in occupation of the Longju outpost and added: "We will take all necessary steps to re-establish our frontier."

Warning to Peking

Mr. Nehru said India had protested to China and warned her that any aggression against the Himalayan States of Bhutan or Sikkim would be aggression against India. He said the Chinese had accused Indian troops of collusion with the Tibetan rebels, but India had replied that there was no truth in this.

"Any country which has to face such a situation has to stand up to it," Mr. Nehru said. "There is no alternative policy but to defend our borders and integrity.

Birmingham Daily Post, Saturday, 29 August 1959

New Delhi, unnerved by the sudden increase of PLA troops on its frontier, immediately deployed increased numbers of its own security forces in the border zones. Sporadic contacts between units from each side of the ill-defined border were inevitable.

After several months of volatile tensions, punctuated by exchanges of fire, the situation eased. In April 1960, a meeting was convened between Prime Minister Nehru and the Chinese foreign minister and veteran negotiator, Zhou Enlai. However, the frosty talks achieved very littler other than to confirm the absence of any common ground between the two antagonists. In what can only be described as a token gesture, both sides entered into a six-month period of lower-level discussions, primarily to compare charts and documentation pertaining to the respective border claims. But it was an exercise in futility as the unbending stance assumed by both sides ensured that there would be no practical basis for a negotiated settlement. New Delhi persisted with its demands that China would have to comply with certain conditions as

Indian Prime Minister Jawaharlal Nehru.

a precursor to any serious negotiations, including a full Chinese withdrawal from Indian-claimed zones. Beijing, however, refused to even consider, let alone accede to, a position that they still found unacceptable.

From this time to 1962, China systematically extended the territory in Ladakh under its control, directly increasing the military threat to Indian forward posts. The Indians responded by commencing limited military operations in Ladakh to force the PLA back, with the objective of restoring the 1956 line, or at least blocking any further Chinese advance.

This 'Forward Policy' employed by the Indians heightened the friction which, allied to a similar scenario in a sector of the northeast frontier, resulted in international attention being drawn to this remote Himalayan tableau.

Claims and counterclaims over their respective territorial rights continued unabated from both New Delhi and Beijing. Both parties appeared to pay scant attention to the realities of the political and psychological situation, concentrating instead on national pride. For India, the colonial legacy that was the McMahon Line set its claims in the northeast in stone, while 'historical tradition', backed up by a miscellany of agreements between Kashmiri and Tibetan authorities dating back to 1684, granted India full entitlement to Aksai Chin. The Chinese also propounded centuries-old 'traditional' rights, adamant also that Tibet never had been independent and had therefore no legal right to enter into any agreements with a foreign power. For Beijing, the Simla Convention could not be recognized as it was without legal foundation.

Western sector Forward Policy deployments.

When weighed up, many believed at the time that India had the makings of a better case but had failed either to promote it effectively or to defend it on the ground. China, on the other hand, had a more questionable legal case, but had masterfully presented the merits of its claims while demonstrating its military prowess to enforce its position.

As the two national forces obstinately squared up to each other, many unanswered questions remained in limbo, negating hopes of a negotiated round-table settlement based on the legitimacy of the McMahon Line, the importance of unique geographic factors such as watershed and crest range, the ethnic and cultural distribution of the border races, and various 'traditional' rights and customs.

Delegates to the Simla Conference, 1913. Lieutenant-Colonel Sir Vincent Arthur Henry McMahon is seated centre.

Hosted by George V, Tibetan guests at Buckingham Palace, June 1913.

By the early 1960s, the Indian Army was still largely equipped with the same Second World War weapons such those used by the Rajputs (*top*) and the 19th Division (*right*) during the Burma campaign. (British Government)

2. HIMALAYAN THEATRE

The dispute along the 700-mile-long eastern sector of the Sino-Indian border, which extends from Bhutan to Burma, covers an area of some 26,000 square miles, including most of India's North East Frontier Agency (NEFA). The NEFA area differed from other sectors of the disputed border territory by its larger size, characterized by the lower but, in many places, extremely difficult and rugged terrain, by dense forests, and inhabited by indigenous tribes numbering several hundred thousand, such as the Daflas, Anataxis, Akas and Monpas.

In sharp contrast, to the west lies the lofty, barren and sparsely populated mountain and plateau country that was in dispute, in Ladakh.

The topographical environment of NEFA is very different from that of contiguous areas to the north and south. NEFA comprises a swathe of steep, hilly and mountainous terrain fifty to a hundred miles wide, rising sharply from the Brahmaputra valley to the crest of the Himalaya. It is deeply incised by innumerable streams whose gullies and valleys, particularly those in the hills adjoining the plains, are choked with heavy vegetation. In places—usually between the outer hills to the south and the high ranges along the border to the north—the rugged terrain gives way to gentler valleys and rolling hills suited to agriculture and tribal settlement. The combination of broken, sometimes impassable terrain and dense vegetation made NEFA almost impenetrable from the plains, hindering adequate internal communications. There was, as a result, a significant lack of central and local administration in this remote area. Added to this, these factors contributed to the isolation and scattering of the numerous tribespeople of NEFA.

That region of Tibet north of the McMahon Line comprises two contrasting types of topography. West of a line drawn approximately north–south from Gyatsa Dzong to Chayul the landscape is typically one of elevated, barren plains and mountains and relatively open valleys lying between 11,000 and 13,000 feet. Endemic flora is sparse, mainly comprising hardy, drought-resistant plants.

To the east, however, Tibet's longest river, the Yarlung Tsangpo (Zangbo in Chinese) and its tributaries have cut deeply into the plateau, dissecting the landscape into a maze of steep-sided ridges and narrow valleys in which streams and rivers flow through narrow gorges. Known as the Brahmaputra where it flows into the Indian state of Assam, at Tsela Dzong (Zela) the Tsangpo flows at an elevation of 9,700 feet before entering a series of great, narrow gorges, where its rapid-filled, cascading

The Friendship Bridge linking China with Nepal, showing the rugged, broken terrain common to what was then known as NEFA. (Photo Felix Dance)

waters swiftly navigate between the mountainous massifs of Gyala Peri (23,930 feet) and Namcha Barwa (25,531 feet). Flowing at an elevation of only 2,000 feet, the Tsangpo now crosses the border claimed by India. At the somewhat lower elevations of the eastern area, heavier rainfall accommodates extensive coniferous forests. A variety of crops, including rice, is cultivated in the relatively low and humid valleys.

Now the Brahmaputra, the river then follows a braided course across the fifty-mile-wide, flat Assam valley. Flooding from June to October every year, the Brahmaputra inundates the surrounding plains to a depth of up to five feet, often blocking transport routes.

The summer monsoon dominates the NEFA's climate, dumping between seventy and a hundred inches on the plains from June to September, although relatively high rainfall also occurs in the pre-monsoonal months of April and May. Into the mountains, precipitation varies considerably according to local terrain, but rainfall generally decreases toward the north.

The Yarlong Tsangpo becomes the Brahmaputra when it crosses into the Indian state of Assam. (Photo Luca Galuzzi)

The driest part of NEFA is in the northwest where the ridges create a rain shadow, blocking some of the summer rainfall. However, there is still sufficient annual rainfall to support moderately heavy vegetative cover.

In Tibet, the openings provided by the north–south alignment of the Brahmaputra and Luhit valleys, allow the monsoon rains to penetrate southeastern Tibet during the summer. Most of NEFA is at such relatively low elevations that cold temperatures and snow as a rule do not present major problems, unlike in the higher passes along the Tibetan border to the north. While heavy snowfalls might block some passes and also the higher stretches of key supply routes for a few days, lower valley routes, such as those along the upper Subansiri tributaries and the Nyamjang River, can be used as alternatives. In March 1959, the fleeing Dalai Lama entered NEFA via the Nyamjang valley route.

On the open Tibetan plains south of the city of Tsethang (Zedang), strong winds in winter and early spring generally prevent any substantial accumulation of snow below the high peaks. In the region of Tibet nearest Towang, however, winter temperatures might fall as low as –18°C, problematic for military campaigning.

In general, winter weather would not be severe enough to stall or prevent military operations for extended periods. Below the high-altitude passes, much of NEFA in winter was conducive to military operations as the streams were then fordable and the land dry.

The rugged terrain and high rainfall also severely restricted both the construction and sustainable maintenance of roads in the frontier area of NEFA by both China and India. The most developed road network in this eastern frontier region was in Tibet, across the border from western Subansiri.

In 1957, the Chinese completed the construction of a road from their main supply and logistics base in the Tibetan capital of Lhasa to Tsethang, a strategic town south of the Tsangpo. With the departure into exile of the Dalai Lama and the upsurge in Tibetan resistance activities associated with the Chinese invasion of Tibet, the Chinese rapidly extended their road network to the south, ultimately connecting the frontier towns of Lhakhang Dzong, Tsona Dzong and Chayul with major Chinese roads farther north. Much of the relatively open terrain along the route is over 12,000 feet. Along the way there is at least one Tibetan pass above 16,000 feet that must be traversed before the frontier towns are reached, making snow and ice a problem during winter.

However, the CIA considered it highly probable that the Chinese would be able to move supplies to Tsona Dzong and forward areas with only brief delays, even during the winter. Compared to other areas, the comparatively efficient logistical system supporting the western sector of the NEFA frontier allowed for the deployment of larger numbers of PLA troops.

To the east the roads were not as well developed, although vehicle routes led to Chayul and Migyitun, across the border from Longju. East of Migyitun, there was no clearly passable access road to the McMahon Line. American intelligence had reported that some Chinese road construction had been taking place near the border on a road running from Linchih along the south bank of the Tsangpo.

A motorable road to Rima, used by the PLA in their successful assault on Walong in the Lohit valley in October/November 1962, is connected to the main Szechwan–Tibet road to the north and with a parallel road from Szechwan to the east. However, all these roads suffered from sporadic seasonal blockages due to landslides and rockfalls caused by the heavy summer monsoons. Farther east and north in Tibet logistical routes for the conveyance of supplies were subject to both landslides in summer and snow and ice in high-altitude mountain passes in winter, making resupply unreliable.

The closest Tibetan airfield to NEFA was located at Tang-hsiung, north of Lhasa and about 200 miles north of the Towang area. It had the capacity to accommodate jet fighters and light bombers.

In general, the inhospitable, rugged terrain and heavy monsoon rainfall in the NEFA hills constrained Indian efforts to construct roads north to their military outposts along the McMahon Line. Except for the relatively new road to Towang, motorable routes did not extend beyond forty miles northward from the plains. As a consequence, frontier outposts had to be supplied by mule train along narrow paths or by airdrop. Resupply by air had become key to Indian military activities in NEFA. In addition, in the 1950s, several small airfields had been carved from the valleys but many of these merely comprised rudimentary strips suitable only for light, single-engine liaison planes and as drop zones. Later airfields were able to take twin-engine aircraft.

The heavy summer monsoons would often disrupt Indian road communications in NEFA. However, whilst the lack of roads and trails, coupled with fast-flowing streams, presented local encumbrances to vehicular movement, such obstacles were also of defensive importance to forces operating in the area. One positive was the prevalent availability of trees, to provide ample material for constructing makeshift bridges.

In 1960, representatives from New Delhi and Beijing met to discuss and document their respective border claims, but neither side could table sufficiently convincing evidence to conclusively prove right of ownership of NEFA in its entirety. All that emerged from the failed deliberations was the reality that the NEFA was a neglected

Indian Air Force DC-3 Dakota airdrop over Walong, NEFA, November 1962. (Photo DPR-MOD)

swathe of real estate that, at the time, lacked any meaningful instruments of central government administration.

Tibet had had some influence in the northwest in and near Towang, arising from the border-straddling of the dominant Tibetan Buddhist faith in the area.

Colonial Britain had also carried a level of sway on the frontier, but such influence had been restricted to the tribal areas of the hills adjoining the plains and did not spread to the loftier, more inaccessible areas to the north. In 1943, in a bid to negate its isolation, Britain launched a programme to assimilate NEFA into the administrative structure of the rest of India. With independence, New Delhi urgently perpetuated this policy of integration as tensions with China along the frontier increased. In a nutshell, the rival parties based the strength of their claims on the legitimacy of the McMahon Line.

The disputed area claimed by Beijing extended to the foothills overlooking the Brahmaputra valley, a tract of territory that ranged up to eighty miles south of the border as claimed by India. In 1960, the Chinese came up with what they believed to be documentary evidence ostensibly revealing Tibetan jurisdiction in the northwestern reaches of the Kameng Frontier Division (pre-independence Sela Sub-Agency), the part referred to as the Monpa area. Centred on Towang, the area is named after the Monpas, an ethnic group whose more than 40,000 members—78 per cent of the district's population—closely resemble the Tibetans in appearance and culture.

Fundamental to the Chinese in relation to its border claim was the fact that the Monpas were Buddhists of the Lamaist (Tibetan) Buddhist faith and that numerous Buddhist monasteries were located in this area. Beijing's contention was that in the past Tibetan administration held control in the Monpa area, and that revenue from taxation was paid into the Tibetan treasury.

India, however, challenged China's rationale by contending that such money was collected for religious purposes only, arguing that this administrative infrastructure was in fact merely the mechanism established and employed by the Lamaist hierarchy, and which was only concerned with spiritual jurisdiction. Beijing also claimed small but indistinct pockets of territory in Lohit. India easily dealt with these claims by reminding Beijing that an official 1914 Chinese document on the limits of Tibet did not include these areas.

For India, on the other hand, the robustness of its claim remained vested in what it regarded as the legally sound McMahon Line that it had inherited from its former colonial master. Political analysts of the time, however, postulated that the veracity of the line in the dispute relied entirely upon whether or not Tibet was an independent state when the McMahon Line was introduced which would in turn determine whether Lhasa had possessed the sovereign and therefore legal instruments entitling it to undertake international obligations and enter into treaty-bound relations.

3. RUSSIAN ROULETTE

In an unpublished report, the Indian Chief of Army Staff from 1962–66, General Jayanto Nath Chaudhuri OBE, said of the growing tensions on the Indian border frontier with Communist China: "It was a game of Russian roulette, but the highest authorities of India seemed to feel that the one shot in the cylinder was a blank. Unfortunately for them and for the country it was not so. The cylinder was fully loaded."

It was apparent from the outset that Beijing appeared to perceive India as neither by temperament nor capability a military threat to its southern border. The first clear indication supporting this came in the autumn of 1950 when, on 7 October, PLA troops entered eastern Tibet and clashed with Tibetans at Changtu.

New Delhi immediately drew Beijing's attention to the harmful effects of this "deplorable" expedition that was heightening tensions on India's borders and proposed, for good measure, deferment of China's admission to the United Nations. A fortnight later, Beijing retaliated by accusing New Delhi of being influenced by foreign regimes "hostile to China and Tibet". Within days, the Indians dramatically toned down their rhetoric, expressing "surprise" at the Chinese allegation, adding that they "only wished for a peaceful settlement" of the situation in Tibet.

Ostensibly placated, China gave New Delhi an assurance, via an Indian delegate at the UN, that their occupation of the nation of the Dalai Lamas would remain "peaceful" and that the PLA corps under the command of Chang Kuo-hua would not venture beyond Changtu (Chengdu) and march on the Tibetan capital, Lhasa. The Indians should therefore not be concerned over the future of Tibet.

Based on this assurance, the Indian UN delegation withheld its plans to censure the Chinese at the UN. In December, Nehru publicly declared, in support of Beijing, that the Chinese position on Tibet should be left to the affected parties to resolve: Beijing and Lhasa.

However, the Chinese reneged on their guarantees when, in May 1951, an agreement with Tibetan representatives, granted the PLA at Changtu the licence to "liberate the whole of Tibet".

Beijing, however, deliberately avoided making any reference to the border disparities between Chinese and Indian maps, thereby ensuring that Nehru would not harbour any antagonistic feelings toward the Chinese presence in Lhasa. Relations remained cordial and Nehru opted for diplomacy rather than sabre-rattling to ensure stability in the region. Chinese diplomacy, largely orchestrated by Zhou Enlai, went

The Tibetan capital Lhasa with the towering Liberation Memorial in the centre. (Photo Pavel Spindler)

to great efforts to convince New Delhi that Communist China "had as yet had no time to revise" the Nationalist Chinese maps.

At the same time, the movement of elements of Indian forces into the NEFA and the establishment of a small number of dispersed checkpoints on the McMahon Line after 1951 was tolerated by the Chinese. Not only were they desirous of sustaining friendly Sino-Indian relations, but the number of Indian personnel involved was militarily of no consequence.

For Beijing, it was imperative for Nehru to be led to believe that the Chinese concurred with the Indian leader's border claims and that they would, therefore, respect the Indian maps. Nehru was thus oblivious to Chinese movements in Ladakh and, in particular, was not aware that, in March 1956, the Chinese had commenced construction work on a new section of the Sinkiang–Tibet road that would traverse the Indian-claimed Aksai Chin region.

It would be twelve months before Beijing made an announcement about the road, albeit deceptively vague, only making reference to the Sinkiang and Tibet terminals and an intermediate location, Shahidulla Mazar. By doing so, Beijing felt comfortable enough to assume that the Indians would understand that the new road would follow the traditional caravan route across the Aksai Plain through Indian-claimed territory.

On 2 September 1957, Beijing announced that the road was weeks away from completion. On the same day, the *People's Daily*, or *Renmin Ribao*, the official newspaper of the Chinese Communist Party, published a tiny sketch map showing that the road cut across the northeast corner of Ladakh. The Indian embassy reported to New Delhi that the road "apparently passes through the Aksai Plain, which is Kashmir territory". Nehru declined to protest to Beijing. As late as 31 August 1959, he defended his earlier decision by informing the Indian parliament of his uncertainty:

Our attention was drawn to a very small-scale map about two and one-quarter by three-quarters inches published in Chinese newspaper indicating a rough alignment of the road. It was not possible to find out from this small map whether this road crossed Indian territory, although it looked as if it did so. It was decided, therefore, to send reconnaissance parties the following summer to find the location of this road.

However, it was not until April 1958 that Nehru made the decision to dispatch two army reconnaissance patrols to assess the road's alignment and to check on the location of Chinese military posts in the Aksai Chin. Regarding this as a personal mission, Nehru ordered the patrols to capture and bring back to the town of Leh any "small" group of PLA they encountered. Should they meet up with a "large" unit, they were instructed to inform the Chinese troops that they were in Indian territory and "ask them to leave".

Two patrols were deployed in June, and in early September one was apprehended on the road by the PLA. On 3 November 1958, Beijing informed New Delhi that the detained members of the Indian patrol would be repatriated, stressing, however, that both patrols had in fact illegally entered Chinese territory. Nehru took this to be a formal Chinese claim to the Aksai Chin, noting on 8 November that it was "now clear, that the Chinese Government also claim this area as their territory". It now dawned on the Indian premier that China's subtle advance into Aksai Chin over an extended period had materialized into the communist state's de facto military control of the disputed territory and that the PLA controlled the Sinkiang–Tibet road and the territory which it bisected.

However, the incident and Beijing's note to New Delhi did little to engender general public awareness of the border issue. In fact, China's claim only resulted in a gradual cooling in the Zhou–Nehru personal relationship. Nehru continued to desist from making any public condemnation of the Chinese intrusion in what he was adamant was legally Indian soil.

He still desired a short-term solution to defuse tensions in Aksai Chin, believing that this could be achieved by common agreement with the Chinese on the ownership

Jawaharlal Nehru on a trip to Beijing, with Zhou Enlai and Madam Sun Yat-sen.

of points along the border at which Indian and PLA patrols occasionally met. Beijing, however, treated Nehru's overtures with circumspection, not wishing to provide him with an opportunity to raise the issue of Chinese claims based on their own maps.

Between December 1958 and March 1959, hitherto cordial exchanges of communications between Zhou and Nehru became increasingly strained, deteriorating into bitterness with the outbreak of the Tibetan revolt on 10 March 1959. With increased media attention focusing on the civil unrest in Tibet, New Delhi was no longer able to restrict all aspects of the simmering border dispute to confidential diplomatic channels. The PLA's military actions against the Tibetan rebels attracted the attention of the Indian media and therefore the public. In parliament, Nehru could no longer underplay, conceal or minimize the seriousness of the border dispute and the resultant worsening of relations with Beijing.

In Beijing, India's commercial attaché told an American official in January 1959 that "India is taking a second look at Communist China", expressing New Delhi's growing discontent with the Chinese. He added that the Chinese had become extremely conceited, on occasion not even acknowledging correspondence from the Indian embassy to the Chinese ministry of foreign affairs. Nehru, however, cautioned

Indian officials about displaying any form of antagonism toward their communist neighbour. He was determined to prevent Sino-Indian relations from deteriorating any further. To this end, he maintained an official policy of non-interference in the Tibetan situation, while handling with circumspection the Dalai Lama shortly after he entered India at Towang on 31 March.

While paying scant attention to New Delhi's diplomatic overtures, Beijing's priority was the crushing of the Tibetan insurrection. The communists were talking and acting from a position of strength: their military superiority over the Indians was substantial. India's rhetoric, therefore, carried next to no weight with the Chinese decision-makers. In April, the Chinese foreign ministry informed the Indian ambassador in Beijing that, in terms of the 1951 agreement between China and Tibet, the latter's autonomy would be respected. In New Delhi, this was interpreted to mean that Tibet would be no more autonomous—as it had been until March 1959—than any of the other so-called autonomous regions in Mao's Communist China.

On 18 April 1959, at Tezpur in the Indian state of Assam, the Dalai Lama, with assistance from Indian Foreign Service diplomat Parappil-Narayana 'P. N.' Menon, issued a statement in which he strongly asserted his resistance to Chinese rule and called for Tibetan independence. Not surprisingly, Beijing reacted sharply, intimating Nehru's duplicity with and being complicit in the Dalai Lama's comments. On 21 April, the Xinhua News Agency, or New China News Agency (NCNA) quoted an extract from a Reuter's dispatch in New Delhi: "The Dalai Lama's statement can have come as no surprise to the Indian Government. It was drafted after several long meetings with Prime Minister Nehru's envoy, Mr. P. N. Menon ... political implications must have been discussed."

Over the ensuing weeks, while the PLA mopped up scraps of Tibetan resistance, Indian leaders faced the realities of Chinese military power with growing concern and trepidation. Foreign Secretary Subimal Dutt told U.S. ambassador Ellsworth Bunker on 27 April that it was impossible for India to fight China over Tibet. If the West with all its arms and logistical clout had not been able to fight for Hungary during the 1956 uprising, he contended that "certainly India could not fight over Tibet which it is practically impossible for Indians even to reach". Dutt admitted that India had only sufficient military capabilities to repel attacks against its own territory. This realization of military impotence introduced an element of fear into official Indian thinking regarding the Chinese.

While maintaining a close eye on the Dalai Lama's secular utterances in the protected Indian environment, the Chinese moved to seal the border with more PLA troops than have ever before been deployed along the frontier. By establishing a significantly enhanced troop presence, it was rapidly becoming evident that Beijing's frontier policy was shifting from that of merely maintaining a few widely scattered outposts, to a policy of sprinkling the entire border with heavily armed 'frontier guards'.

As part of this tactical exercise, in July and August 1959, PLA troops seized all arms, ammunition and packhorses belonging to Bhutanese infantry units. The diminutive Himalayan state immediately called on New Delhi to protest this violation of "traditional Bhutanese rights and authority". On 25 August, Nehru reminded parliament that, in terms of the 1951 treaty obligations to defend Bhutan and Sikkim in the event of any threat to their sovereignty, India had a right to act on foreign policy matters pertaining to Bhutan. Reluctance to act, however, was not well concealed.

By mid-June, Indian frontier reports reflected a sharp falling off in the flow of Tibetans crossing into India, indicating that the PLA was now in a position to block virtually all border passes. The reports drew attention to intensive Chinese activity to improve their lines of communication by constructing 'jeepable' roads to the principal passes all along the border and by upgrading existing mule and pony trails. Of particular concern to the Indians was mention in a report that the Chinese had nearly completed the Lhasa–Yatung (Yadong) road, thereby extending the road network right up to the Indian border. It was believed that this would be passable for jeeps, and within three years, be upgraded to accommodate heavy vehicles.

Estimates of troop dispositions on both sides of the border showed that, by late summer, PLA troops outnumbered Indian forces in all sectors. At least one sector was manned by lightly armed Indian border police and not by regular Indian Army units. The uniformed Indian presence was mainly tasked with intercepting Tibetan rebels entering Indian territory and disarming them. It would now only be a question of time before the close proximity of greater numbers of armed Chinese and Indian personnel along the border resulted in clashes.

By mid-June, Indian patrols were reporting frequent cross-border forays by PLA troops in pursuit of Tibetan rebels. Such penetrations, however, were generally not deep and withdrawal by the intruding troops almost immediate. New Delhi, therefore, remained reluctant to lodge any sort of formal protest with Beijing.

The first known Chinese border infringement happened on 15 June in the eastern sector when a group of Tibetan rebels was intercepted while attempting to cross the border into India and engaged by PLA troops. However, the first serious contact between Chinese and Indian troops came to light in Beijing's note of 23 June in which they charged that in excess of 200 Indian troops had infiltrated, shelled and seized the Migyitun village area of Longju in Chinese territory on the eastern sector. The Chinese went on to allege that the Indian forces has acted in collusion with Tibetan rebels ensconced there.

New Delhi refuted the charges three days later, maintaining that all Tibetan 'refugees' were disarmed as soon as they crossed into Indian territory, adding that India

A Tibetan rebel.
(Photo U.S.A.F.)

was not in any way responsible for rebel activities in the Migyitun area. Nevertheless, the Chinese remained convinced that, as Indian patrols became more active along the border, they were aiding and abetting rebels in recrossing into Tibet.

This was followed by two further minor incidents on 28 July and 7 August. The first occurred in the western sector when a six-man patrol of Indian police was disarmed and taken into custody by a twenty-five-strong PLA detachment near Pangong Lake, Ladakh. However, they were released three weeks later in the interests of 'friendship' following a formal Indian protest.

The other took place in the eastern sector when a PLA force of 200 crossed into Indian-claimed territory at Khinzemane on the disputed McMahon Line, forcing back an Indian unit on patrol in the area. In an official protest on 11 August, New Delhi pointed out that, by crossing the east–west-running Thag La Ridge, the Chinese troops had crossed into Indian territory "as the boundary runs along the Thag La Ridge". This claim would have a more profound outcome in 1962.

In the annals of the Sino-Indian border dispute, the first armed clash between Chinese and Indian troops occurred on 25 August in the eastern sector. In an exchange of fire between a PLA troop detachment and a twelve-strong Indian picket in the area south of Migyitun, four Indians were taken prisoner. The following day, an undetermined number of PLA troops outflanked Longju before opening fire and forcing the Indian troops to flee their post.

New Delhi's protest of 28 August was suddenly far less conciliatory in tone, accusing the Chinese of "deliberate aggression". The Indians pointed out that "until now" New Delhi had observed a "discreet reticence" over Chinese border actions, but these now constituted an issue "which is bound to rouse popular feelings in India". It was now very apparent that Nehru perceived the August transgressions as the last straw and anticipated a public outcry.

Addressing a vociferous parliament on 28 August, the Indian premier voiced caution against being "alarmist" and "indulging in shouting and strong talk".

Parliament members, however, were not subdued as they expressed their anxiety over the incidents and Chinese intentions along the entire border. The Indian legislature had now largely become impervious to Nehru's policy of appeasement toward the Chinese: could bombs be dropped to chase the PLA out of the NEFA? If India failed to defend its own sovereignty then what would be the fate of small Asian countries that looked to India for guidance?

Nehru remained unruffled in the face of baying MPs but reassured the house that any aggression against Bhutan and Sikkim would be considered as aggression against India. Responding to a suggestion from the floor, Nehru stated that he would be prepared to initiate a white paper on Chinese border infringements. In so doing, he was able to stall abrasive condemnations of the Chinese, but the clamouring in parliament and the press started to manifest themselves. As time progressed and public anti-Chinese sentiment spread, Nehru came under increasing pressure to deliver on the government's pledge to resist Chinese incursions along the border with Tibet.

In the field, the Indians faced a dilemma in their needs to strengthen the border posts of the Assam Rifles in NEFA. A shortage of men acclimated to operations at high altitudes presented a major stumbling block. Kashmir was the only immediate source of reinforcements, but there was an understandable reluctance to weaken the forces facing India's other hostile neighbour, Pakistan.

Against this scenario, Nehru's non-belligerent stance on China prevailed: "We have to be friends with the powerful country with whom we have a border

Armed confrontation. Chinese and Indian troops in a face-off on the border.

of 2,680 miles." He remained opposed to conducting military operations against Chinese border posts south of the McMahon Line. Instead, he sought a resolution to the dispute in two international directions. Firstly, he let the Soviet Union know of his predicament with the People's Republic of China. The Kremlin's silence on the PLA's heavy-handed quashing of the Tibetan revolt had not gone unnoticed in New Delhi. U.S. Ambassador Bunker was simultaneously made aware of the Indians' concerns.

Hoping to persuade Soviet leader Nikita Khrushchev to exert pressure on Beijing to desist from further border incursions, New Delhi instructed the Indian ambassador in Moscow to discuss the deteriorating situation with Khrushchev in person. Mention must be made of the fact that Beijing had not responded to a number of notes from India. Their only response had been to start "an insidious propaganda against India among socialist and nonaligned countries".

In early September, Indian Foreign Secretary Dutt privately warned the Soviet and Polish ambassadors that if Chinese border violations were to continue, then India would have no choice but to review its policy of nonalignment.

Khrushchev, however, refused to take sides, in spite of supplying military equipment to India. It would take a statement by the Soviet news agency TASS on 9 September to reflect the Kremlin's undeclared stance in the Sino-Indian border crisis: the Soviet Union would maintain its policy of neutrality when "a bloc country [is] in a dispute with a non-bloc country".

Nehru's second choice of action was an appeal to Beijing for settlement negotiations, spurning calls from some MPs for strong action against the Chinese who were "behaving as at war". Nehru placed great importance on for settlement through discussion of "small border disputes" over "a mile or two" of territory. For the Indian premier, Aksai Chin was all "barren land ... and not worth fighting for". Negotiation was the desired instrument to settle territorial ownership.

Responding to Nehru's open invitation to a negotiated settlement, China's Zhou Enlai elucidated Beijing's position, which can be summarized as: 1) China did not recognize the McMahon Line in the eastern sector that was the result of a surreptitious arrangement entered into between British and Tibetan representatives and quietly

Aerial view of the Nepal–Tibet border region. (Photo Christopher Michel)

appended to the Simla Treaty in 1914. No Chinese government had ever ratified the treaty. However, in what could only have been an insincere gesture of conciliation, Zhou offered, for the sake of goodwill and peace along the border and a negotiated settlement of the border dispute, the fact that "Chinese troops have never crossed that line"; 2) India had to admit that the Tibet–Uttar Pradesh border in the middle sector has never been delineated; 3) In the western sector where the Ladakh region borders with Sinkiang and Tibet, Beijing only recognized the "traditional customary line" as the boundary. This line had its origins in historical tradition and Chinese maps had always drawn the boundary conforming with this line; 4) China's border with the Himalayan states of Sikkim and Bhutan was not considered to be part of the current dispute. China has always respected the "proper" relations between them and India.

On 19 October, Zhou personally wrote a letter to Nehru, suggesting that Indian vice-president Sarvepalli Radhakrishnan visit the Chinese capital that would "serve as a starting point for negotiations". However, three days before the Chinese ambassador to New Delhi delivered Zhou's letter, on 24 October, elements of the PLA clashed with an Indian border police patrol near the Kongka Pass in southern Ladakh, killing nine and capturing ten. Nehru and Radhakrishnan had no choice but to reject Zhou's offer.

Beijing repudiated any culpability in the Kongka Pass incident. A month earlier, an editorial in the *People's Daily* of 16 September had already commented that India had "dispatched troops to cross the border and occupy more than 10 places belonging to China". The editor went on to suggest that the India "withdraw its troops quickly from the Chinese territory they occupied recently".

By October, it had become evident that PLA troops along the border were following orders to inform Indian units to withdraw. Indian military intelligence was aware that elements of the PLA had repeatedly arrived at the Khinzemane Indian outpost in NEFA between 9 and 11 October to warn elements of the Assam Rifles for the "last and 17th time" to withdraw or face being pushed back by force within days. Border posts in Bhutan and Sikkim had also come under similar threat.

Despite Nehru's strong aversion to military action on the frontier, on 12 October Foreign Secretary Dutt succumbed to pressure from the Indian Army to move troops onto the border.

Elite Indian troops would be deployed along the NEFA–Tibet border: Jats, Gorkhas, Sikhs and Rajputs.

However, the Kongka Pass clash in Ladakh on 21 October did not involve regular Indian Army troops—even though Beijing referred to the dead and captured as "soldiers"—but rather poorly armed and equipped border police. In what can only be described as a one-sided engagement, the fact that the Indian policemen lost

Nehru meets *jawan* troops, 1962. (Photo DPR-MOD)

nineteen killed and taken prisoner, would indicate overwhelmingly PLA numbers or firepower, or both.

A 23 October an NCNA release in Beijing claimed that Chinese frontier guards had been compelled to retaliate in self-defence against Indian "armed personnel more than 70 in number, after disarming three Indians on 20 October". The next day, a statement from the Indian External Affairs Ministry, in a contradictory version of the incident, claimed that PLA troops entrenched on an overlooking hilltop position had suddenly opened heavy rifle, mortar and grenade fire on a border police search party looking for two constables and a porter who had failed to return from patrol on 20 October. The statement added that, in spite of returning fire, the Indian police were overwhelmed by Chinese numerical strength and weaponry.

The Indians, including General Thimayya, believed that it would be extremely dangerous to weaken the Pakistan border to man the entire border with China. A decision was therefore taken to draw from the reserve forces in the Punjab without touching key deployments in Jammu and Kashmir.

The first divisional movement of Indian troops into the border area subsequent to the October Kongka Pass incident, was the redeployment of the 4th Division, stationed in reserve at Ambala (Punjab) to Missamari (Assam) in the Kanleng division of NEFA. Headquartered at Tezpur, the division was tasked with manning existing and any additional posts on the western half of the NEFA border. Fearing that the

INDIA SENDS MORE TROOPS TO FRONTIER

MR. NEHRU URGED TO RETHINK POLICY

Party Says "Throw Chinese Out"
Reinforcements were moving up yesterday to the Indian outpost involved in last week's clash with Chinese troops. Indian newspapers criticised Chinese actions and called for a reappraisal of policy toward China. According to usually well-informed sources in New Delhi, a detachment of Indian troops has set off from an army base in Eastern Ladakh to reinforce the police checkpoint at Tsogtsanu, three or four days' march distant, where the clash occurred. Further reinforcements will be sent by air, and mule-trains with supplies will also set out for the forward area from Leh, Ladakh's capital—about a fortnight's march from the scene of the fighting.

A public meeting in New Delhi last night under the auspices of the Right-wing Jan Sangh Party demanded that Chinese forces be "thrown out" of Indian territory. A resolution said that the Ladakh incident was "part of planned aggression all along our Northern frontier and must be taken as a calculated challenge to our country's sovereignty and territorial integrity."

China has informed India that seven of the 17 Indian border police reported killed in the clash are alive and in Chinese hands. A note received from the Chinese Government by the External Affairs Ministry yesterday added that the Chinese had also recovered the bodies of nine Indians. This means that one Indian is still missing. The Chinese Note said they had also arrested three members of an Indian party on the previous day.

India has claimed that the clash took place 40 to 50 miles inside Indian territory. China, which claims 4,000 square miles of Ladakh territory, countered that Indian troops had deliberately violated Chinese frontiers and launched an "unwarranted armed attack on Chinese frontier guards."

Birmingham Daily Post, Monday, 26 October 1959

departure of the 4th Division had left that section of the border with Pakistan vulnerable, the Indians immediately set about raising a new division—the 17th—at Ambala.

At this point in time, while considering his military options and still regarding Ladakh as wasteland, Nehru made the unpopular decision of allowing the Chinese annexation of Aksai Chin to go militarily unchallenged. Accepting the situation as a fait accompli, Nehru could now invest all available resources in maintaining the status quo on the rest of the border with China. Media and public condemnation of the Indian premier's unpalatable writing-off of Aksai Chin, including student demonstrations in New Delhi on 4 November as part of the 'Throwback the Aggressors Day'. In the space of two months, India had been humiliated by two military defeats.

As 1959 drew to a close, Zhou Enlai once more offered New Delhi a conciliatory resolution to the border conundrum. In a note to the Indians, Zhou stated that since the October clash, the PLA was no longer sending out patrols. He invited Nehru to a personal meeting to roadmap negotiating parameters and the way forward. Zhou intimated that Beijing would be willing to forfeit its claim to the region south of the McMahon Line in exchange for New Delhi withdrawing its claim to Aksai Chin.

Early in February 1960, Nehru advised Zhou that he was amenable to a preliminary meeting, but one in which any form of negotiation was absent. He went on, though, to invite Zhou to New Delhi to "explore every avenue for a settlement". To the amazement of New Delhi Zhou agreed to visit at the head of a high-level delegation.

However, and despite intensive private one-on-one discussions, Zhou's six-day visit to the Indian capital in late April totally failed to achieve any of his objectives. Nehru remained steadfast in his requirement for the withdrawal of all PLA troops from what India saw as occupied areas of Ladakh.

Clearly, Zhou had underestimated Nehru's obstinacy and had completely miscalculated his ability to exploit the Indian leader's apparent Gandhi-style philosophy of peaceful resolution to conflict. Nehru rejected Zhou's offer of further meetings, adding that he had no intention of limiting Indian patrols along the frontier. Further discussions in 1960 proved as fruitless.

In January 1961, the Chinese foreign ministry monthly stated that it was Mao Zedong himself who provided the general principle of diplomatic forbearance for the period: "In 1960, Chairman Mao again instructed us repeatedly that in our struggle, some leeway must be provided for the opponent." This, specifically constituted an integral part of Mao's dual policy of 'unity and struggle' toward India. But in India, there was a growing consensus that China was becoming India's prime enemy and their Maoist policy meant nothing but 'struggle'. So, while the Chinese leaders, including Mao, at this time believed that there remained opportunities for future

People's Liberation Army on parade, 1959.

diplomatic jostling with the Indians, New Delhi no longer brooked any such diplomatic recourse.

From late 1959, New Delhi had started to lodge formal protests with China about alleged Chinese air force violations of Indian air space, claiming that these had occurred in the previous two months along the whole border area. On 4 April 1960, the Indian Ministry of External Affairs despatched a similar note protesting Chinese overflights of Indian territory in the previous three months. Beijing did not respond but Nehru had personally raised the issue during Zhou's visit to India toward the end of April. Later, while visiting West Berlin, Nehru had confided in Mayor Willy Brandt that Zhou had challenged him to shoot down any aircraft violating Indian airspace, then the Indians would then see that the aircraft did not belong to Communist China.

New Delhi, however, was not convinced, and on 22 August 1960, another note was sent to Beijing, protesting fifty-two known violations of Indian airspace since March, the Chinese aircraft approaching from Tibet.

Three weeks later, Beijing broke its silence on the issue, refuting all Indian claims that the Chinese air force was violating Indian airspace. A spokesman in the Chinese foreign ministry then wrote to New Delhi giving the "real facts":

In the early days of April 1960, the Indian government informed the Chinese government that aircraft had been discovered flying over the Sino-Indian border area. During his visit to India in April, Premier Zhou Enlai told Prime Minister Nehru in their talks on April 25 that it had been found through investigations by the Chinese government that these were U.S. aircraft. They took off from Bangkok, passed over Burma and China, and crossed the Sino-Indian border to penetrate deep into China's interior to parachute Chinese secret agents, weapons, supplies, and wireless sets, and then flew back to Bangkok, again passing over the Sino-Indian border.

Premier Zhou Enlai assured Prime Minister Nehru at the time that the Chinese government would never allow its aircraft to fly over the border and said that the Chinese government had sent a note to the Burmese government stating that should Burma discover any unidentified aircraft in its airspace, it was fully entitled to take any countermeasure: either force them to land or shoot them down. China would do likewise should it discover such aircraft in its own airspace.

By not accepting Zhou's assurances in April, the note went on to accuse the Indians of "a very unfriendly act" toward Beijing. However, New Delhi refused to accept the contention that the aircraft involved belonged to the United States, saying as much in a further letter of protest on October. Further written protests followed on 13 February and 29 April 1961, 10 and 24 March, and 25 July 1962. The last violation, according to New Delhi, took place over Chushul, a village in the Leh district of Jammu and Kashmir. The Indian protests went unanswered, Beijing satisfied that its September 1960 statement was adequately clear as China's stand against the Indian allegations.

In 1961, Beijing's policy toward India remained based on the Maoist contradictory assumptions: the necessity of uniting with Nehru while simultaneously struggling against him. The Chinese hoped that a window for negotiations would present itself, but, at the same time, noting that Nehru would only talk about an unconditional PLA withdrawal from Aksai Chin.

Beijing, increasingly frustrated by Nehru's now dogmatic insistence on a total Chinese withdrawal as a precondition to any bilateral border deliberations, would need a different approach to bring the Indian premier to the negotiating table. In pursuance of this, in April 1961, the Chinese informally sounded out the mood in New

Shenyang J-5 (Chinese-built MiG-17 type) at the Datangshan China aviation museum, Beijing. (Photo Calflier001)

Delhi to ascertain if Nehru would be amenable to third-party arbitration. The following month, the Burmese were approached to persuade Nehru to negotiate on the China–Burma–India border junction. Burma declined the Chinese request. All the while, Beijing was tacitly absorbing Indian accusations, insults and snubs without publicly retaliating or defending it actions.

The Chinese had no desire to remain indefinitely embroiled in a territorial dispute with no closure. Anti-Chinese sentiment in India was now of some concern to Beijing, allied to the fact that other eyes were now closely watching unfolding events along the Indian frontier, not least of all Moscow.

Three years after the death of Stalin in 1953, his successor, Nikita Khrushchev, denounced Stalin's crimes and propounded a policy of 'destalinization'. However, Mao Zedong, an adherent of Stalinism and a practitioner of the Soviet model, accused the new Soviet leader of revisionism. A yawning ideological chasm developed between Moscow and Beijing, resulting, in 1961, in Communist China's formal denunciation of Soviet Communism as the product of "revisionist traitors". The outcome became known as the 'Sino-Soviet split', which marked the commencement of Communist China and the Soviet Union vying with each other for the status of vanguard to lead the international revolution of world communism.

Adverse public opinion in India, Beijing therefore believed, might provide Khrushchev with ammunition with which to rally support from other communist states against Communist China's expansionism in the region. In order to spread dissension, the Chinese opted to move beyond Mongolia, Burma and Nepal, and early in 1961 proposed border talks with Pakistan, India's much-loathed and dangerous northwestern neighbour.

However, all this achieved was the further alienation of New Delhi, angry with Chinese attempts at wooing Pakistan into the Chinese camp. Nehru further entrenched his single, all-pervading precondition: no withdrawal, no negotiations. While India's top military commanders adopted an uncompromising hard-line approach, including military operations against Chinese posts, the Indian parliament's pressure on Nehru was incessant. The leader's perceived intransigence was now pushing MPs toward the army generals' way of thinking: the employment of force to oust the PLA from what was regarded as Indian soil. It was inevitable that Nehru would buckle. He yielded under the burgeoning weight of parliamentary and military consensus calling for India to flex its military muscle.

From April 1961 on, Chief of General Staff in the Indian Army, Lieutenant-General Brijmohan Kaul, instructed all three army commands to provide ten per cent of their existing troop strengths for service with border units. Explaining the rationale to his commanders that his intention was not to deploy entire units but to augment those army units already on the border in a manner that would not give the Chinese reason to increase their own troop strengths. The general, a Sandhurst graduate, was also eager to avoid giving the press the impression that the Indian Army was massing troops on the frontier. New Delhi, for good reason, was equally wary of Beijing's intelligence network in the region. A PLA soldier, who had been apprehended in Bhutan in March, had been tasked to establish contact with Indian military personnel to obtain critical order of battle information.

Nehru showed increased concern during June that the Chinese were preparing to react to Indian troop movements by launching an all-out attack. However, the edge was taken off his anxiety when Indian intelligence reported in June and July that the Chinese were simply working on improving their border posts and lines of communication.

Frustrated with its inability to budge Nehru from his hard-line stance on Chinese withdrawal from Aksai Chin as a precursor to negotiations, Beijing adopted a different approach by emulating the Indians' practice of constantly lodging formal border infringement protests.

The first in a litany of formal protests came in August against Indian military advances arising out of Lieutenant-General Kaul's orders in April. Following charges

Indian Air Force Canberras, 1961. The English-built aircraft was commonly employed in a reconnaissance role.

of Indian air reconnaissance sorties conducted over Chinese-claimed territory in May and June, Beijing's first note in the series, dated 12 August 1961, complained that:

1. Since last April, Indian troops had begun to infiltrate into China's Demchong area.
2. In May Indian troops set up a checkpoint at nearby Oga.
3. In June, a detachment of Indian official personnel established themselves at Wuje (Bara Hoti).
4. In July thirty heavily armed Indian troops carried out two patrols as far as Charding La.*
5. Also in July, Indian troops patrolled well past the Thag La Pass.

New Delhi's counter claims and Nehru's public statement in response were concise: Indian troops were deploying on Indian soil. At this point, an open Sino-Indian exchange was the most acrimonious since 1959, when Nehru addressed the fifth Indian white paper in parliament. In an attempt to prevent any further criticism of his soft-touch policy, for the first time Nehru expressed an option to strike at any belligerency that threatened India's sovereignty. He confidently indicated that India's recent strengthening of its border defences had now in fact tipped the military situation on the frontier in India's favour. Nehru was clear: "We will continue to build these things up so that ultimately we may be in a position to take effective action to recover such territory as is in their possession." He seemingly

---

* *la* is Tibetan for pass.

boasted by adding that, while the Chinese had set up three new posts in Ladakh, India had established six, including one at Daulat Beg Oldi near the Karakorum Pass in northwest Aksai Chin. Some of Nehru's statistics, however, appeared ambiguous, but his tone was not.

The Indian Director of Artillery added to the process of extolling his nation's military prowess when, in late November, he informed the U.S. military attaché in New Delhi that his forces in Ladakh possessed the firepower to make the Chinese posts untenable.

Beijing denied that the PLA posts were new. It said all were within Chinese territory. The Chinese contended that the post at Nyagzu had been there for a long time, while denying that they had ever established a post at Dambuguru.

Nehru's public comments, combined with outrage from parliament and extensive press coverage, produced a noticeable change in Beijing's tone. For the first time it was conceivable that Nehru was bolstering his military presence on the border to retake territory in the western sector by force. In response, the Chinese immediately launched a massive propaganda campaign aimed at deterring India from any such plans.

Early in December, the Chinese foreign ministry publicly pointed out that, since May, they had dispatched four notes to New Delhi accusing the Indians of overstepping the lines of actual control in the western and middle sectors. Indian statements in November, the Chinese continued, amounted to an open admission that India was intentionally and unilaterally preparing to usurp the balance of power on the border, to be followed by an imminent, further invasion of Chinese territory. Nehru's 28 November address to parliament was overwhelming evidence that India's expansive programme of road and building construction was in preparation for the use of force to settle the border stalemate. To the Chinese, New Delhi's chosen policy was extremely dangerous. Beijing declared that it was not intimidated in the slightest by India's posturing and threats of force. It would retaliate against any Indian invasion.

In a 9 December note, New Delhi added to the increasingly acerbic rhetoric by stating that what the Chinese had done in Aksai Chin since 1956, the Indians could do better in 1961.

By February 1962, the Chinese had gradually eased up on their anti-Nehru propaganda attacks. In what had become an endless and increasingly confusing cycle of threat and talk of conciliation, Beijing reminded the Indians that it was still amenable to a political settlement of their territorial differences. Chinese embassy officials in New Delhi informed journalists of a tranche of proposals which included joint Sino-Indian use of the Chinese-built Aksai Chin road, the establishment of a joint commission to delineate the Ladakh border, and China's acceptance of the legality of the McMahon Line. New Delhi, however, remained insistent that Chinese withdrawals from Indian-claimed areas was an imperative before it would even consider looking at any proposals that Beijing may have formulated.

By April, with unsustainable internal criticism of his 'soft' policy, allied with Beijing's propaganda campaign which Nehru took to be aimed at him personally, the battered Indian premier embarked on a military option that, in essence, would be to besiege forward Chinese posts in the western sector.

Formulated in December 1961, the military strategy incorporated the establishment of five new Indian posts, each of about a company strength of a hundred troops, behind nine existing forward PLA posts in Ladakh west of the 1956 Chinese claim line. It was intended for the posts to be manned all year round. Defence Minister V. K. Krishna Menon tasked the Indian air force with compiling a detailed report of its ability to operate sustainable logistical support by air.

In a cabinet subcommittee briefing in late December, Nehru rubber-stamped the plan. Krishna Menon stated that the new posts would be sited so as to cut off the Chinese lines of supply to their forward posts, with the objective of starving out of the Chinese and forcing them to evacuate their posts, after which Indian troops would take up residence in the posts. Such bases would then facilitate the launching of reconnaissance patrols close to the road.

Beijing warned India that Indian troop movements must not compromise the frontier status quo.

Whether through intelligence or intuition, Beijing reacted, but they preferred not to publicly challenge the Indians with counteraction. In late January, the Chinese ambassador to Cambodia 'privately' told his Burmese colleague that Zhou was still desirous of talking to Nehru talks, but if New Delhi wanted to "bully, pressure or fight" the Chinese over disputed borders, they would discover the Chinese to be tough adversaries who were capable and willing to use force to resist attack. The threat was communicated to India's ambassador in Phnom Penh, who passed it on to New Delhi.

Early in February, New Delhi's reaction was also 'private'. The Indian high commissioner in Karachi told a U.S. embassy official in the Pakistani capital that, notwithstanding the fact that India now had adequate military forces in Ladakh to defeat PLA troops in the border area, they did not want armed retaliation from the Chinese that would almost certainly precipitate a major conflict. New Delhi would assure that all operations would be strictly limited and restricted to Ladakh. The Indian diplomat, however, made sure to tell the American that Beijing would find it logistically onerous to reinforce its forward PLA units.

Early in April 1962, the Indians commenced operations, with the immediate tactical objective of outflanking PLA forward posts, thereby forcing the Chinese to withdraw to the 1954 line. In mid-April, two Indian Army battalions were deployed to outflank and eventually 'retake' the PLA post in the Chip Chap River area. This post had been specifically targeted as the Indians were adamant that it was new, despite the Chinese arguing that it had been in existence for a long time.

By month's end, Beijing formally protested that, in the period from 11 to 27 April, the Indian Army had established two posts, one southwest and one northwest of their PLA post, and had encircled it with groups of up to 120 troops. In a note dated 28 May, the Chinese charged that the Indian flanking operation included the establishment of a third post some five miles southwest of their post, in addition to conducting aggressive patrolling in areas immediately to the west, northwest, and southwest. On 29 April, the U.S. military attaché in New Delhi confirmed that the Indian Army had commenced operations by deploying two battalions to the disputed border area of Ladakh.

China reciprocated by repositioning its army along its claimed Aksai Chin border sector running from Karakorum Pass in the north, southward to the Kongka Pass, a flat distance in excess of a hundred miles. The Chinese issued a terse warning to whoever cared to listen that Indian military operations might trigger the PLA to engage

PLA troops of the 1960s.

in combat. When asked by the U.S. embassy on 2 May precisely what had prompted Beijing's threatening note of 30 April, the reply from the director of the China Division of India's Ministry of External Affairs (MEA) was mendacious: perhaps it arose from "present Pakistani pressure on India in the United Nations Security Council".

Prime Minister Nehru was now following the roadmap of his own design: placate internal public fears of an imminent Chinese invasion, while giving substance to his more recent promise of resorting to military options. On 2 May, he publicly asserted that the Chinese note would not in any way deflect him from supporting the forward policy of troop augmentation along the border in Ladakh: "We will stay where we are [and are] prepared for them if they step up patrolling."

On 3 May, Nehru, in a statement to parliament, told the house that he had found nothing alarming in Beijing's threatening note of 30 April, dismissing it merely as China's reaction to his military initiative in Aksai Chin. The army had set up a number of posts, some of which were to the rear of a Chinese post, causing Beijing "some annoyance".

New Delhi chose to ignore China's threat, and on 1 May Indian Army headquarters, with Nehru's approval, ordered the immediate dispatch of 1,800 troops to Ladakh. The troops were drawn from the Srinagar Command, based in and named after the

Indian position, with Bren light machine gun, on the disputed border. (Photo Hindu Archives) Indian troops ferry supplies by mule.

56

INDIAN ARMY NOW FACES ITS FIRST BIG TEST

By Maj. General Richard Hilton[*]

The open trial of strength between China and India, so long expected, seems to have commenced in earnest. Each side accuses the other of aggression, after the custom of modern diplomacy, but the point is really immaterial.

It is a waste of time to argue any longer about legitimacy. China, not being a member of United Nations, cares not a rap for that body or its resolutions. Armed force alone can settle this quarrel.

Advantages
It is easy to foresee what China hopes to gain. If by next spring she can push the Indian Army clear of the mountain defiles, Chinese engineers, with unlimited coolie labour, may be able to extend their military roads southward to the beginning of the Indian plain. A proper large-scale invasion of India would then no longer be an impossibility.

As the opposing troops stand at present, China has all the advantages of supply and transport facilities. Her new military roads across Tibet bring lorry columns to within a few miles of the front, whereas Indian supplies must be manhandled a hundred miles or more across country unfit even for mules.

This, of course, brings in the air question. If this were an all-out diplomatically recognised war, the Indian Air Force could do much to counteract the Chinese advantage of lorry roads versus coolie paths. Air attacks take a heavy toll of lorries moving across the vast treeless plateaux of Tibet.

But unfortunately for India, her fighting commanders are hamstrung by similar political inhibitions to those which prevented General MacArthur from attacking across the Yalu [River on the North Korean–Chinese border]. Indian politicians, pathetically maintaining the diplomatic fiction that this was not "war", have forbidden any warlike action against "Chinese territory" that they wrongly and feebly admit Tibet to be. Once more the fighting men have to subordinate sound military action to political daydreams.

Coventry Evening Telegraph, Tuesday, 23 October 1962

---

[*] Major-General Richard Hilton was Brigadier General Staff, Allied Forces, Norway, at the end of the Second World War. He then served as deputy head of the British Military Mission to the Soviet Zone, Germany, before being appointed military attaché to the Soviet Union. He retired in 1948.

largest city and the summer capital of the Indian state of Jammu and Kashmir. Their deployment of 2 May, after a 'fight-to-the-death' speech of encouragement by General Kaul, was as a supporting force in any fighting that might erupt as a result of the Chip Chap operation. That same day, Kaul sent signals to those Indian border posts which were tactically close enough to retaliate immediately if the PLA took any of the new Indian forward posts by force.

General Kaul's 'strike back' licence to his troops cemented India's commitment to a military solution to the long-standing border dispute.

On 6 May, the Chinese chargé d'affaires in New Delhi said that he was shocked by India's army advances in Aksai Chin where new posts were established "at places deep within China's territory". China was now left with only one option: resist. He concluded: "I hope the Government of India realizes the consequences that are bound to follow."

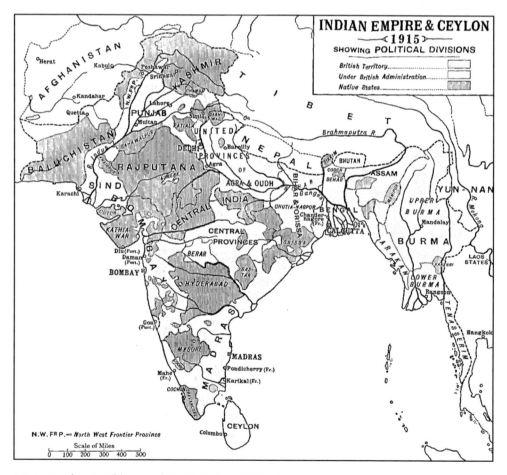

Vincent Arthur Smith's map of British India, published in 1920.

U.S. President John F. Kennedy welcomes Prime Minister Jawaharlal Nehru to America at Andrews Air Force Base (*top*), and, along with with First Lady Jackie Kennedy, Nehru's daughter and future Indian prime minister, Indira Gandhi, seen here holding a bouquet (*below*), November 1961. (Photos Abbie Rowe)

Above: From left: Prince Norodom Sihanouk of Cambodia, Indian defence minister V. K. Krishna Menon and Soviet foreign minister Andrei Gromyko, Thirteenth Session of the General Assembly function, 1958. (Photo Government of India)

Left: Pakistani Prime Minister Huseyn Shaheed Suhrawardy and Chinese Premier Zhou Enlai signing the Treaty of Friendship between China and Pakistan, Beijing, 1956.

4. THIS IS OUR MOUNTAIN

"One cannot possibly seriously think that such a state as India, which is militarily and economically weaker than China, would really launch a military attack on China."
Central Committee of the Communist Party of the Soviet Union, 6 February 1960

In the military expression of Nehru's 'forward policy', the Indian Army's resources were lacking. In Ladakh there were only two battalions of the Jammu and Kashmir Militia. There were no regular troops and no logistical or tactical support. Within the western sector there were no roads either into the area or within it. Allegations of gross corruption had stalled the construction of the Srinagar–Leh road, so Leh remained accessible only by mule trail or by air. Landing strips only existed at Leh and Chushul, which meant everywhere else in the sector relied on airdrop supplies.

In addition to the two locally raised militia battalions, Western Command at the time estimated a requirement for a brigade group, comprising five battalions. Indian intelligence suggested that the PLA in the sector were at regimental strength, with supporting armour. The Chinese road network was at an advanced stage. Western Command had called for the deployment of four battalions in 1960, and one in 1961.

India, however, continued to suffer from a failure to relate political decisions and commentary to military realities. Responding to Nehru's statement to parliament early in 1961 that the military advantage in the western sector had now swung in India's favour, the sector XV Corps commander, Lieutenant-General S. D. Verma, felt compelled to say something. In a letter to Chief of Army Staff General Pran Nath Thapar, Verma pointed out that the situation on the ground did not reflect the prime minister's assurances to parliament. The consequences of proceeding with military advances based on illusions of superiority carried the potential of disastrous consequences.

Soon thereafter, Verma paid a severe price for daring to challenge the political establishment: Lieutenant-General L. P. 'Bogey' Sen was appointed General Officer Commanding-in-Chief, Eastern Command, and Lieutenant-General Daulet Singh the same for Western Command. Being sidelined, Verma resigned immediately.

But soon Verma's assessments and predictions of the balance of power in the western sector started to haunt the military. Western Command had required five infantry battalions by late 1961, but only one battalion, the 1st Battalion, 8th Gorkha Rifles (1/8 Gorkhas), had been inducted to augment the two militia battalions. 114 Brigade headquarters was established at Leh, from where posts and picquets were set up, all within Indian-claimed territory, except the one at Demchok which was inside the Chinese claim line. One post was set up at Karakorum Pass, named Daulet Beg Oldi, but this was also not in territory claimed by the Chinese.

Operations took place at altitudes of between 14,000 and 16,000 feet in Arctic conditions. Winter clothing was both inadequate and in short supply. The rarified air, caused by lower air pressure at high altitudes meant that troops could only manage small loads and pack-mules were as ineffective. As a consequence, all supplies, often including water, had to be airdropped.

In an election campaign speech in support of defence minister Krishna Menon in January 1962, Nehru continued to ply his boasts of an all-powerful Indian Army:

> I say that after Mr Menon became the Defence Minister our defence forces have become for the first time a very strong and efficient fighting force. I say it with a challenge and with intimate knowledge. It is for the first time that our defence forces have a new spirit and modern weapons.

The reality was, at that time, the Indian Army was short of 60,000 rifles, 700 antitank guns and 200 2-inch mortars. Stocks of artillery shells were critically low. Five thousand field radios were required, together with 36,000 batteries. Based on the fact that pre-1948 army vehicles were obsolete, the army's transport capabilities were

PLA soldiers with Type 56 light machine gun (Soviet RPD).

short of 10,000 each of one-ton and three-ton trucks. Two regiments of tanks were inoperable for want of spares.*

Nehru continued to display an ebullient persona to the Indian public well into mid-year 1962. His forward policy had seen the establishment of army forward posts either overlooking PLA positions, or on tracks and roads to their rear. He put across a confidence that the Chinese would soon be forced to withdraw, while brushing aside Beijing's persistent warnings of grave consequences.

In June, the 5th Battalion (Phillora Captors), Jat Regiment (5 Jats), was inducted into Ladakh, bringing the western sector strength to four battalions. The Jats were also broken down into small posts and patrols. By mid-summer, some sixty Indian forward posts now faced what had grown into a full PLA division that outnumbered Indian forces by five to one. The PLA's other significant advantage was that they were able to move by truck, while the Indians had to walk everywhere.

The PLA units all possessed standard supporting arms, including the Type 56 7.62mm light machine gun (Soviet RPD), while the whole Indian 114 Brigade only had one light machine-gun platoon for support, equipped with the Enfield, .303 Bren

light machine gun, the standard infantry support weapon of the British Army in the Second World War.

The Chinese were equipped with Type 56 automatic assault rifles, a 7.62mm variant of the Soviet-designed AK-47, and Type 56 semi-automatic carbines of the same calibre. The Indian Army, however, had to contend with the Lee-Enfield, .303-inch bolt-action, magazine-fed rifle— generally the SMLE Mk III used by military forces of the British Empire and Commonwealth in the Second World War. First World War-vintage .303s were not uncommon.

Indian soldier with Lee-Enfield .303 bolt-action rifle.

* Statistics from Neville Maxwell's *India's China War* (Jonathan Cape, 1970).

(Photo No. 1 Army Film & Photographic Unit)

The rustic Indian Army posts, accommodating a platoon or sometimes a section, featured linked weapons scrapes, often only a few inches deep as the ground was frozen solid, even in summer. Wholly dependent on airdrops for resupply, the troops lived in a miscellany of tents and crude makeshift shelters knocked together from packing cases and parachutes.

In what became known in Indian Army circles as the Galwan incident, Nehru's handling of the crisis enjoyed unprecedented vindication. Maps at brigade headquarters in Leh showed the Galwan River valley in Jammu and Kashmir as one of the best routes for the movement of troops into Chinese-held areas in Aksai Chin. Since around 1959, the PLA had had a post at Samzungling at the head of the valley. Identifying the strategic value of an Indian Army post facing off the PLA post, particularly to prevent the PLA from making a significant advance into Indian-claimed territory, General Kaul ordered Samzungling to be one of the first forward moves. Sector commander General Daulat Singh hesitated, firmly believing that the recommencement of PLA patrols from their well-established post at Samzungling would inevitably result in an undesirable confrontation between

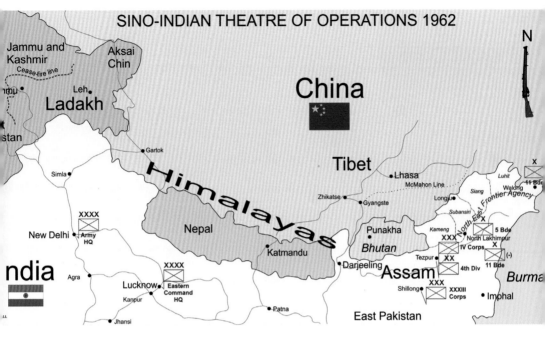

SINO-INDIAN THEATRE OF OPERATIONS 1962

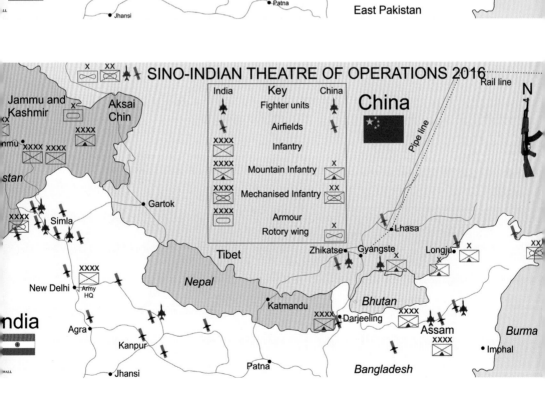

SINO-INDIAN THEATRE OF OPERATIONS 2016

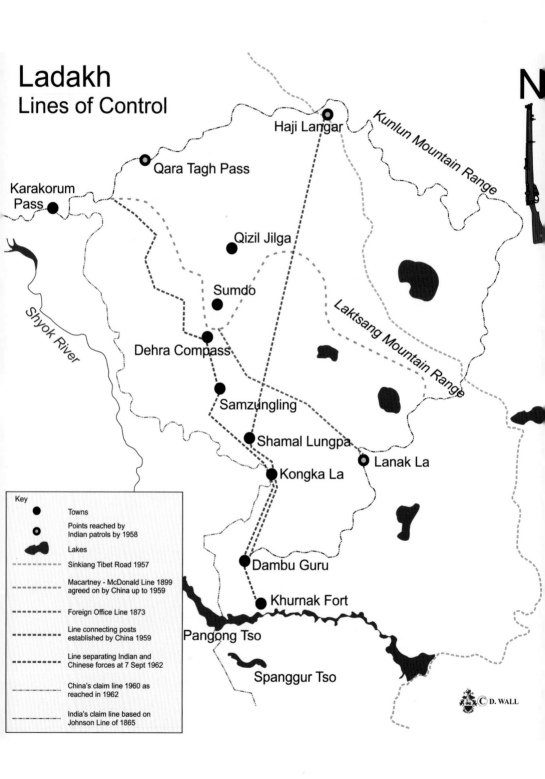

Ladakh
Lines of Control

N

Haji Langar

Kunlun Mountain Range

Qara Tagh Pass

Karakorum Pass

Qizil Jilga

Sumdo

Laktsang Mountain Range

Shyok River

Dehra Compass

Samzungling

Shamal Lungpa

Lanak La

Kongka La

Dambu Guru

Khurnak Fort

Pangong Tso

Spanggur Tso

© D. WALL

Key

● Towns

◉ Points reached by Indian patrols by 1958

Lakes

Sinkiang Tibet Road 1957

Macartney - McDonald Line 1899 agreed on by China up to 1959

Foreign Office Line 1873

Line connecting posts established by China 1959

Line separating Indian and Chinese forces at 7 Sept 1962

China's claim line 1960 as reached in 1962

India's claim line based on Johnson Line of 1865

Battle of Thag La Ridge 1962

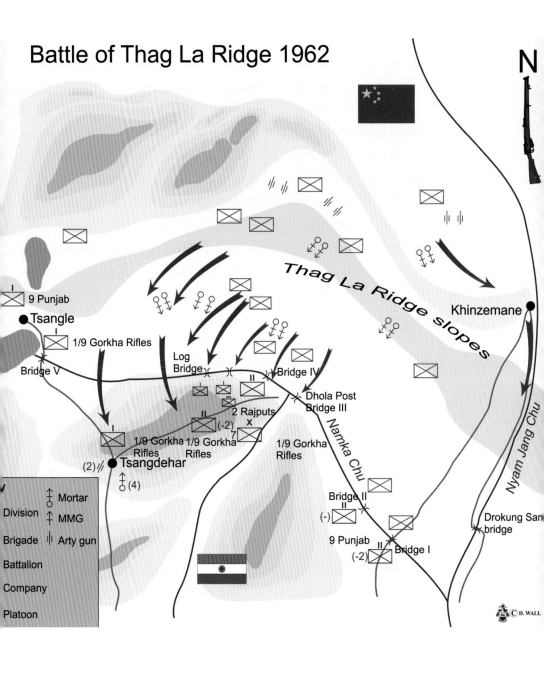

N

Thag La Ridge slopes

Khinzemane

9 Punjab
Tsangle

1/9 Gorkha Rifles

Bridge V

Log Bridge

Bridge IV

Dhola Post
Bridge III

2 Rajputs

1/9 Gorkha Rifles   1/9 Gorkha Rifles

Tsangdehar

(2)

(4)

1/9 Gorkha Rifles

Namka Chu

Nyam Jang Chu

Bridge II

(-)

Drokung San bridge

9 Punjab

(-2)   Bridge I

Division   ↕ Mortar

Brigade   ↑ MMG

Battalion   ‖ Arty gun

Company

Platoon

© D. WALL

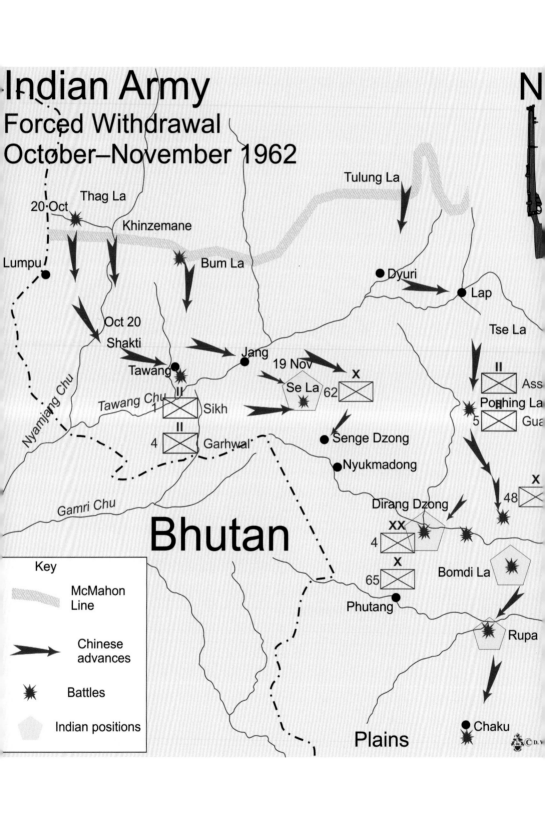

Indian Army
Forced Withdrawal
October–November 1962

N

Tulung La

Thag La

20 Oct

Khinzemane

Lumpu

Bum La

Dyuri

Lap

Tse La

Oct 20
Shakti

Jang

19 Nov

X

Tawang

Se La

62

II

Ass

Poshing La

Tawang Chu

1

Sikh

5

Gua

II

4

Garhwal

Senge Dzong

Nyamjang Chu

Nyukmadong

X

Gamri Chu

Dirang Dzong

48

Bhutan

XX

4

X

65

Bomdi La

Phutang

Rupa

Plains

Chaku

© D. V

Above: Dirang Dzong on the Bomdi La–Se La road. (Photo Kunal Dalui)

Below: The Himalaya, Ladakh. (Photo Karunakar Rayker)

Above: Tawang War Memorial. (Photo Kunal Dalui)

Below: Chinese President Xi Jinping (left) and Indian Premier Narendra Modi, September 2014. (Photo Narendra Modi)

Above: PLA Type 96a, or ZTZ-96, second generation main battle tank. (Photo Vitaly V. Kuzmin)

Below: Indian Arjun third generation main battle tank. (Photo Hemantphoto79)

एम बी टी अर्जुन मार्क - I
MBT ARJUN MK - I

Above: Indian Air Force Sukhoi Su-30 Mk I. (Photo Chris Lofting)

Below: PLA Air Force Chengdu J-10. (Photo Retxham)

Indian and Chinese forces. Kaul disagreed and, overruling Daulat Singh, sent in a platoon of Gorkhas from Hot Springs. After a month of trekking over inhospitable mountain ridges, the resilient Gorkhas arrived at the upper reaches of the Galwan on 5 July. Taking up a commanding position, the Indians were able to isolate a PLA post farther downstream. They also held up a small Chinese supply team. Three days later, Beijing dispatched a note of strongest protest, demanding an immediate withdrawal of Indian troops, warning that China "will never yield before an ever-deeper armed advance by India, nor give up its right to self-defence when unwarrantedly attacked".

On 10 July, the Indian post faced a company of PLA troops advancing on their position in assault formation. The numbers rapidly grew to battalion strength as the Chinese approached to within a hundred yards of the Gorkhas. Using interpreters and loudspeakers, the Chinese played on the Gorkhas' Nepalese patriotism, claiming that China was a better friend to Nepal than was India. They berated the Gorkhas for misguidedly serving India's expansionist designs in the region. Weapons cocked, the Gorkhas would not be intimidated.

In New Delhi, the Chinese ambassador was summoned and warned that if the PLA troops moved any closer to the Indian post at Galwan, the Gorkhas were under orders to open fire. If the Chinese actually launched an attack on the post, India would retaliate in like manner against Chinese posts.

Over the next few days, the PLA withdrew a short distance, but maintained an encirclement of the Indian post to deter any resupply by land. Western Command accordingly sought an aerial resupply from New Delhi, explaining that to do so by land would provoke a clash with the PLA, and was therefore not an option. For New Delhi, however, this was a perfect opportunity to exploit the moral initiative gained when the Chinese pulled back, albeit only marginally so. A land resupply was ordered to challenge the PLA siege. As it transpired, the small force turned back in August when threatened by a far superior PLA force that they would open fire if the Indian resupply group moved an inch further in the direction of the Galwan post. Western Command reiterated that land resupply was beyond the army's capabilities. The Gorkhas' position was supplied by air from then until 20 October when it was annihilated.

Nehru was suddenly in a very confident and buoyant mood. His forward policy had been tested in a face-to-face stand-off and had succeeded. A pro-Nehru Indian journalist lauded the Indian premier's success at Galwan as "a unique triumph for audacious Napoleonic planning". Others were not so convinced. A respected Indian political columnist, with very useful army contacts, wrote in August that the PLA enjoyed a ten-to-one superiority in the western sector, with all the added advantages of topography and lines of communication.

Indian Air Force Douglas DC-3 Dakota used to airdrop supplies to troops at posts inaccessible on the ground.

On the back of the Galwan incident, parliament now clamoured for equally bold measures to forcefully push the Chinese out of Aksai Chin. Members of the opposition were particularly vocal, questioning why, if the ruling party had repeatedly told Lok Sabha—as the Indians refer to their parliament—that the military had the upper hand in the western sector, did they not order a massive and immediate operation to push the Chinese invaders off Indian soil. In August one MP stated that "the bogey of Chinese superiority should not worry our military experts". Another declared that "two hundred Indian soldiers are equal to two thousand of the Chinese. Why are we afraid of them? Why are we not able to hurl them back?" The same MP, swept up in patriotic jingoism, contended that if government gave the call to arms, in six months "a well-trained army of four million Hindus will march to the Himalayas and throw back the whole Chinese force".

On 26 July, New Delhi dispatched a note to Beijing which, surprisingly to many, was conciliatory. Political commentators of the time put this down to the presence on a visit to New Delhi of the Soviet first deputy prime minister, Anastas Mikoyan. Nehru attached great importance to Soviet sympathy for India's position in its border dispute with China. Moscow was urging a negotiated settlement, so hosting the second-most powerful figure in the Soviet Union presented an ideal opportunity for Nehru to show Khrushchev that he was fully complying with Soviet wishes.

The Indian parliament was outraged, describing the note as "a most shocking and surprising document". The *Hindustan Times* in its 10 August edition openly attacked the Indian government under the heading 'The Road to Dishonour':

The Government of India in its infinite wisdom has deemed the time opportune for a complete reversal of its China policy. It has all but sanctified the illegal gains of Chinese aggression in Ladakh as the price for the opening of a new round of negotiations with the overlords of Peking. In so doing it has broken faith with the people of India—the people and its parliament.

American Senator John F. Kennedy's call in 1959 for increased support for India's five-year plans largely reflected U.S. policy toward India: "if China succeeds and India fails, the economic development balance of power will shift against us." Notwithstanding the now President Kennedy describing Nehru's visit to Washington in November 1961 as "the worst head-of-state visit" and his meeting with him "like trying to grab something in your hand only to have it turn out to be just fog", the U.S. stood firmly behind India in its quarrel with China.

Following a three-year period of calm since the Longju incident in August 1959, Nehru's forward policy now also impacted on the eastern sector. In December 1961, Eastern Command had received orders from army headquarters to advance posts as close to the McMahon Line as feasible, and to establish new posts to achieve total and effective occupation of the whole frontier. Patrols, mutually suspended soon after Longju, should recommence between posts but they faced the same tactical and logistical problems as those of their comrades to the west. Reaching the McMahon Line took weeks of arduous trekking over very difficult terrain, and all supplies had to be airdropped.

In February 1962, General Kaul was compelled to go to Assam to personally address protests from the corps commander, Lieutenant-General Umrao Singh, who had major reservations about setting up posts along the McMahon Line. With the assistance of intelligence officers, Kaul then used maps to specify sites for the new posts and, in the first half of 1962, the Assam Rifles established twenty-four new posts along the McMahon Line.

The PLA was unconcerned about the fresh arrival of Indian troops, as long as they remained on their side of the McMahon Line. Potential flashpoints, however, existed where the actual alignment could not be agreed to by the two sides, such as the hamlet of Longju. But Thag La Ridge would become the crucible of the 1962 border war between India and China.

On 24 March 1914, Britain and Tibet signed off on a map which depicted the western extremity of the McMahon Line terminating on the border with Bhutan. However, when Indian surveyors conducted an exploratory expedition into this northwestern corner of NEFA in the 1950s, they discovered that, in the absence of a watershed to follow, McMahon had, according to the Indians, drawn his line some three to four miles south of a prominent ridge in the vicinity of Thag La. In August

1959, recognizing McMahon's error, the Indians established a post at Khinzemane, north of the McMahon Line shown on their maps.

That same month, about 200 PLA troops pushed the dozen or so men of the Assam Rifles out of Khinzemane. Two days after the Chinese withdrew the Indians returned to their post. Again, the PLA arrived to remove them, but this time, the Assam Rifles stood their ground, causing the Chinese to seemingly accept the Indian presence. An acrimonious exchange of notes ensued between New Delhi and Beijing with both claiming ownership of an area of about twenty-five square miles.

By mid-1962, the Indian Army eastern sector order of battle formed by Nehru's forward policy appeared like this:

INDIAN ARMY HEADQUARTERS, NEW DELHI
   Chief of Army Staff: General P. N. Thapar
   Chief of the General Staff: Lieutenant-General B .M. Kaul
   Deputy Chief of the General Staff: Major-General J. S. Dhillon
   Director of Military Operations: Brigadier D. K. Palit

A section of the indistinct and therefore disputed Sino-Indian border. (Photo Sandrathomas)

EASTERN COMMAND HEADQUARTERS, LUCKNOW
  General Officer Commanding-in-Chief: Lieutenant-General L. P. Sen
XXXIII Corps Headquarters, Shillong
  General Officer Commanding: Lieutenant-General Umrao Singh
IV Corps Headquarters, Tezpur
  General Officer Commanding: Lieutenant-General B. M. Kaul
4th Infantry Division Headquarters, Tezpur
  Commander: Major General N. Prasad
5 Infantry Brigade Headquarters, North Lakhimpur
  Three battalions spread out in NEFA
7 Infantry Brigade Headquarters, Tawang
  Commander: Brigadier J. Dalvi
  1/9th Gorkha Rifles
  9 Punjabs
  2 Rajputs
11 Infantry Brigade, Nagaland

The PLA order of battle was largely formed from the seven combat and two logistic commands—more than 200,000 troops—deployed in the subjugation of Tibet. For the PLA, it was a major training exercise, as Chairman Mao explained, "to harden out troops to combat readiness." Reporting on the battle of Mitika in August/September 1959, General Ding Sheng stated: "This battle not only ensured

The PLA Infantry Division 11, reflecting on the tactical lessons learned from engagements in Tibet, reported that "It has been proved by many experiences that carrying out encirclement is the most effective method to wipe out large numbers of rebel bandits." Later, when the division summarized the effective tactics used in the border war, 'encirclement' was the first mentioned.

In a 2008 article on the suppression of the Tibetan uprising, Chinese National Defence University Professor Xu Yan pointed out that the biggest difference between the PLA and the Indian Army in October/November 1962 was the "combat quality of officers and soldiers. Most of the troops of the Liberation Army who fought at the China–India border have a glorious history; besides that, they had also acquired rich combat experience in high and cold mountain regions". The two PLA field commanders employed in the border conflict were both veterans of the Tibetan suppression.

Tibetan soldier, 1938.
(Photo Bundesarchiv)

the safety of transportation on Qinghai–Tibet Highway, it also gained us experience of fighting with the large unit encircling tactic and carrying out policies in
pastoral regions."

Some of the principal elements of the PLA command structure included:

PEOPLE'S LIBERATION ARMY HEADQUARTERS, BEIJING
   Chief of Joint Staff: General Luo Ruiqing
TIBET MILITARY COMMAND ADVANCE COMMAND POST FOR CHINA–INDIA
BORDER SELF-DEFENCE COUNTER-ATTACK (ABB. ADVANCE COMMAND POST,
CODENAMED Z419), LHASA THEN TSONA
   General Tan Guansan
   Political Commissar General Yin Fatang
   Regiments 154, 155 and 157

PLA Ground Force, eastern sector
  Field commander: Lieutenant-General Zhang Guohua
  Field commander: Lieutenant-General Ding Sheng
Fifty-fourth Army
  Division 130
Lanzhou Military Command
  Infantry Division 11
  Artillery Regiment 308
  Engineers Regiment 136
Shannan (Lhoka) Military sub-Command
  Regiment 1

Arriving at the China–India–Burma border trijunction on 4 June 1962, a patrol of the Indian Army Assam Rifles ignored their maps, treating the Thag La Ridge a few miles to the north as the McMahon Line boundary. A site just south of the small Namka Chu River, called Che Dong, was selected for a new Indian forward post. There was not a single PLA soldier anywhere to be seen. By calling the position Dhola Post, the platoon commander, an army captain, opened the door to a complex string of confusing issues.

Even though the new Indian position was in direct contravention of India's 1959 agreement with Beijing not to alter the status quo in the Thag La Ridge area, New Delhi insisted that, as a matter of national policy, Dhola Post would remain. However, at Tezpur, 4th Division headquarters, Major-General Prasad was deeply concerned about the ramifications of setting up a military post within what his maps showed as Chinese territory. Dhola Post had, from its initial siting, become a tactical liability.

Prasad's fears of a Chinese armed reaction gained added credibility when a wooden sign was discovered close by, proclaiming in Chinese: 'THIS IS OUR RIVER AND OUR MOUNTAIN'.

An uneasy calm settled over the area, until 8 September when a force of around sixty PLA troops suddenly descended Thag La Ridge. The post commander had deviously reported the Chinese strength at 600, in the hope that this would galvanize brigade headquarters to immediately render assistance. But the PLA did not press home an attack, electing instead to set up positions that commanded the Indian post.

That same day, Nehru had left for London to attend a Commonwealth prime ministers' conference and, in his absence, defence minister Krishna Menon convened a meeting the next day with generals Thapar and Sen in the defence ministry in New Delhi. General Kaul was not in attendance, but Cabinet Secretary S. S. Khera was present. The meeting made the decision to immediately and with force evict the Chinese from Indian-claimed territory. Krishna Menon's far-reaching decision was unilateral, in which he did not follow protocol by convening a meeting of the Cabinet Defence Committee. The action would be codenamed Operation Leghorn.

The generals were told to ignore their maps regarding the McMahon Line in the Thag La area. A signal was passed to XXXIII Corps at Shillong to immediately move the 9th Punjab Battalion to Dhola Post, with the remainder of 7 Brigade to follow within forty-eight hours. All troops had to be kitted out in full combat gear, and should attempt to encircle the Chinese troops investing the post.

On 12 September, General Sen travelled to Tezpur to personally convey the defence ministry's orders to corps commander Lieutenant-General Umrao Singh, and General Officer Commanding the 4th Division, Major-General Prasad: the Chinese must be thrown back over Thag La Ridge.

In the early hours of the 14th, troops of the 9th Punjab started out from Lumpu for Dhola Post. The battalion, however, was at half strength and could only muster 400 rifles. The second battalion of the brigade, 1st Sikhs, was stationed at Dirang

Indian position, NEFA, 1962. (Photo DPR MOD)

Dzong as it could not be accommodated at Tawang. The remaining battalion, 1/9th Gorkhas ready for a break from three hard years in NEFA, was turned around and redeployed into the Thag La area.

On 15 September, the Punjabis were ordered to capture Thag La and take up positions at two passes at 16,000 feet. But due to a delay in the signal arriving, by this time the Punjabis were spread out along the deep, fast-flowing Namka Chu on a front of several miles. With the main PLA strength waiting to the north of the ridge, and the Punjabis carrying only fifty rounds of ammunition each, Brigadier Dalvi "flatly refused to obey this order and informed Divisional H.Q. accordingly. G.O.C. agreed with [him] and protested to XXXIII Corps, who in turn asked Eastern Command to have the order countermanded".

The Punjabis had a choice of two routes to the Namka Chu. The shorter route through Hathung La, at an altitude of 13,500 feet demanded steep climbs, with the porters having to use ropes to ascend with their heavy loads. The porters would take three days, while the hardened Punjabis managed within twenty-four hours, but at the expense of doing so without adequate supplies of food and ammunition, and having to leave behind heavy support weapons, mortar bombs and digging tools. The biggest disadvantage of using this route was that the Indians trekked directly under the noses of their Chinese adversaries. The second option was via Karpo La I, which approached Dhola Post from the south. At 16,000 feet, this route entailed hazardous climbing rather than marching. Both routes were devoid of any cover, forcing the Indians to tent in the open. Their 'winter' uniforms were not manufactured to withstand snow and sub-zero temperatures.

By now the Punjabis were spread out over almost seven miles, the equivalent of a two-day march. Two companies were positioned at the two lower bridges—I and II—downstream from Dhola Post. A third company was positioned at Bridge III close to Dhola Post. The battalion commander had also deployed a platoon to the commanding 14,500-feet Tsangdhar. So scattered were the Punjabis that they would not be able to support each other in the event of an attack by the PLA. The tragic reality was that the troops were incapable of attacking, let alone defending in any depth: they might only be able to stop casual trespassing.

Across the Namka Chu, the PLA were keeping pace with very little effort. The Indians estimated that, by the 15th, they were facing two PLA infantry companies, positioned between the Namka Chu and the ridge. These were joined by a third company the following day, while Indian intelligence placed a PLA battalion at Le, just north of the ridge. By the 20th, there had been a significant increase in PLA strength in the area: two regiments (equivalent to an Indian Army brigade), divisional artillery and, twenty miles back at Tsona Dzong and virtually linked by road to Thag La, the rest of the division. Concentrations of Chinese troops had also been

An Indian light machine-gun (LMG) bunker, NEFA, 1962. (Photo Kunal Dalui)

seen at Bum La, east of Khinzemane. It is important to note, however, that at this time both the civilian Intelligence Bureau and the army's military intelligence were inept and unreliable.

In New Delhi, parliament was not sitting, resulting in a dangerous situation of various government personnel talking independently to journalists, assuring them that the situation at Thag La was being well managed, and that India would not allow Chinese advances along Thag La to go unchallenged. Allied to this, Eastern Command's General Sen told civilians that the whole of 7 Brigade would be in place on Namka Chu and ready to strike at the Chinese on Thag La by 21 September. This was yet more evidence of poorly informed and ill-advised spreading of baseless optimism, or naivety. It would only be at the start of October that more troops arrived to bolster the Punjabis on the Namka Chu: one company at that.

At XXXIII Corps, General Umrao Singh remained incalcitrant. He was not prepared to commit his troops to a combat situation in which they could not win and could not be adequately supplied.

Arguably, of greater concern was the infrastructural absence of any semblance of written communication, especially orders. Orders from Army Headquarters and Eastern Command were often orally by telephone. Generals would also receive verbal orders while attending strategic meetings in New Delhi. With Nehru and Krishna Menon out the country, Chief of Army Staff General Thapar desperately needed finite written confirmation of India's commitment to ousting the Chinese from Thag La by force. Within hours, the general received what he was after, a written order signed by junior government official S.C. Sarin: "The decision throughout has been as discussed at previous meetings, that the Army should prepare and throw out the Chinese as soon as possible. The Chief of the Army Staff is accordingly directed to take action for the eviction of the Chinese in the Kameng Frontier Division of NEFA as soon as he is ready."*

XXXIII Corps commander, Lieutenant-General Umrao Singh, remained unconvinced of Operation Leghorn's chances of success, and on 29 September he submitted his concerns to Eastern Command: his orders were impossible to implement and General Officer Commanding-in-Chief Lieutenant-General L. P. Sen's handling of the operation was lacking in competence. This left Sen and Thapar with a dilemma. Umrao Singh's refusal to follow orders warranted immediate dismissal but without him the operation would flounder even before it was launched. Sen put forward Major-General S. H. F. J. Manekshaw's name to Krishna Menon to take over command of XXXIII Corps from the obstinate Umrao Singh. However, just the sheer suggestion that the general who had only recently been charged with disrespecting him was anathema to the fuming Krishna Menon. Instead, it was agreed that a new corps under a new commander be raised to take over operations.

In yet another unprecedented move, on 3 October, Chief of General Staff at Army HQ, Lieutenant-General B.M. Kaul, was appointed General Officer Commanding the new corps, designated IV Corps. However, it was not lost on many that Kaul had never been in command of troops in a combat situation, but Thapar and Sen had high expectations that Kaul would mollify the Indian public by executing a successful Operation Leghorn. With the situation now extremely volatile along the Namka Chu, New Delhi and Beijing failed to reach agreement on the agenda for a last-ditch attempt at a negotiated settlement.

Leaving New Delhi with public fervour ringing in his ears, the *Times of India* extolled Kaul's military virtues by describing him as "a soldier of extraordinary courage and drive". Arriving at Tezpur on 4 October, accompanied by hand-selected officers, Kaul assumed command of IV Corps, a unit that still only existed on paper.

---

* The Kameng is the most westerly of the five divisions that make up NEFA and is the division where Thag La is situated.

INCREASED ALARM ON CHINESE AND INDIAN FIGHTING

Diplomatic observers in China and India are taking a serious view of the border situation where skirmishing has taken place intermittently throughout the summer, but not before on the present scale. Continued fighting in the disputed border area between China's Tibet region and India's north east frontier was reported in a brief communiqué carried by all Pekin newspapers today. The communiqué said one Chinese officer was killed and three soldiers were wounded in fighting yesterday near Chedong village which the Chinese say is on the Tibetan side of "the so called MacMahon line". Indian casualties were not reported.

"Situation Critical"
The communiqué said Indian troops opened fire, threw hand grenades and destroyed part of the Chinese defences, forcing the Chinese to take defensive measures. The last editorial comment was when the Pekin "People's Daily" said: "The situation is most critical and the consequences will be serious. Let the Indian authorities not say that warning has not been served in advance." Newspapers reported that China had lodged with India "the weightiest and strongest protest" over a clash in the area and demanded its immediate evacuation by India. The "Times of India" says nine Chinese were believed to have been killed in "by far the most serious clash that has so far taken place between Indian and Chinese troops and it is too early still to foresee its final outcome.

Deliberate Act
"The Chinese have deliberately chosen this sensitive sector to precipitate the latest clash because they are evidently determined to extend the conflict to the borders of Bhutan as well. "Present skirmishes around Chejao Bridge can and might easily develop into a major battle if the Chinese start reinforcing their positions with fresh troops."

Coventry Evening Telegraph, Tuesday, 25 September 1962

Kaul declined Umrao Singh's offer of staff officers from XXXIII Corps, as he knew they would have shared their commander's negativity about Operation Leghorn. Indian Army dispositions when Kaul arrived were:

NAMKA CHU
9th Punjab Battalion (9 Punjabis)
One 2nd Rajput Battalion company (2 Rajputs)
One machine-gun platoon (two guns)

LUMPU
7 Infantry Brigade HQ
Two 2nd Rajput Battalion companies
1/9th Battalion Gorkha Rifles (1/9 Gorkhas)
4th Battalion Grenadiers (4 Gren)
One heavy-mortar troop
Remainder of the machine-gun company
Some engineers

TAWANG
1st Sikh Battalion (1 Sikh)
4th Battalion Garhwal Rifles (4 Garhwals)
Some guns and heavy mortars of 4 Artillery Brigade

REST OF NEFA
Five understrength 5 Infantry Brigade battalions.

Nehru meeting Indian Army officers at Charduar, 1962. (Photo DPR-MOD)

On 5 October, Kaul flew to Lumpu by helicopter, where he read the riot act to the brigade major: expedite Operation Leghorn orders or be discharged from the army. Perceiving the officer's complaint that only about thirty per cent of the airdropped supplies could be retrieved as yet another delaying tactic, Kaul snapped, "Retrieve or starve."

The very next day, 1/9 Gorkhas and 2 Rajputs marched out for Thag La, attired in cotton uniforms, each man with a blanket and fifty rounds of ammunition. The troops passed through the 16,000-feet Karpo La I Pass, before descending 1,500 feet to Tsangdhar where they halted to await further orders.

Kaul then flew to Serkhim to meet with Major-General Prasad, commander of the 4th Infantry Division, for a situation briefing. Kaul, now better appraised, signalled Army HQ and highlighting the difficulties they were facing. There was a heavy PLA build-up below Thag La Ridge, the PLA equipped with artillery, heavy mortars, medium machine guns, recoilless rifles and automatic assault rifles. However, Kaul assured New Delhi that he was committed to launching Operation Leghorn on 10 October. Due to the sheer strength of the opposition he was about to take on, Kaul strongly proposed that the Indian Air Force (IAF) be placed on alert to provide immediate offensive air support if—and when—the situation demanded it.

A Gorkha soldier operating a No. 31 radio set, NEFA, 1962. (Photo DPR-MOD)

The only flat areas that could accommodate helicopters were north of the Namka Chu, so to reach Dhola Post, on 6 October Kaul and his party set off on foot through the Hathung La Pass. Like most of the troops, Kaul also struggled in the rarified air, and for part of the way he was carried on the back of a tough Tibetan porter.

Soon after lunch on the 7th, Kaul arrived at Dhola Post, where he was shocked at what he saw. The deep Namka Chu was still flowing swiftly through the heavily wooded valley, through which troop movement would be difficult and fields of fire restricted. On the Indian side of the river the terrain rose gradually for about 500 yards before rising sharply 4,000 feet above the valley floor to the Tsangdhar airdrop zone on the crest of the Hathung La Ridge. On the northern, Chinese-held side, the rising ground was much narrower before rising—in some places precipitously so—to the crest of the Thag La Ridge. From what Kaul could discover that afternoon was the existence of a hill feature—Tseng-jong—beyond the north bank of the Namka Chu that commanded and outflanked the PLA positions opposite Dhola Post on the southern slopes of Thag La Ridge. Tseng-jong would be a strategic imperative, and Kaul decided that he would stay with 7 Brigade until the operation was over.

The following day, 8 October, Kaul initiated Operation Leghorn by moving 2 Rajputs and 1/9 Gorkhas down from the natural defensive position on Tsangdhar east to assume staging positions at bridges III and IV on the Namka Chu. The troops would only reach the line the next day, the 9th.

That same day, at a briefing with his senior officers, including Prasad and Dalvi, Kaul gave one of the more questionable orders of the operation: the next day—New Delhi's stipulated date for the commencement of operations—2 Rajputs must move to the 16,000-feet Yumtso La Pass on the western crest of the Thag La Ridge. From here, they would have a commanding position of the PLA troops on the south-facing slopes, effectively entrapping them against the Namka Chu. However, such a reckless deployment would be in plain sight and close proximity of the Chinese, which all the officers, except for Kaul, believed would trigger a massive PLA retaliatory response. If, by some remote chance the Rajputs succeeded in attaining Yumtso La, they would perish from cold and starvation. Brigadier Dalvi would later recall that moment: "A variety of astonished gazes greeted Kaul's announcement. General Kaul at first had the smug look of a conjuror holding the rabbit by the ears, later he had a look of defiance as if daring anyone to question his orders." Kaul, after dismissing Dalvi's and Prasad's misgivings, conceded to first sending out an exploratory patrol before committing the whole battalion.

At around midday on 9 October, a patrol made up of fifty Punjabis crossed the Namka Chu, reaching Tseng-jong without incident at last light. Upon their arrival, the patrol commander dispatched a section with a Bren gun onto Thag La Ridge itself to cover the patrol's flank.

The Bren gun, seen here manned by Indian soldiers in the Second World War, remained the Indians' standard infantry-support weapon for decades after the war. (Photo Vanderson)

Kaul was ecstatic. He was right, and the pessimists were all wrong, describing them as "bloody fools". In a lengthy signal Kaul boasted that bold and speedy tactics had caught the enemy unawares, representing a good start to clearing the Chinese off Thag La Ridge. His troops were already securely positioned on the ridge, but he failed to concede that it was only a small section that had made it to the top. He concluded by saying that morale, upon the troops receiving the positive news, was very high on the Namka Chu, even to the extent that a Sikh soldier had stood up with Bren gun at the hip, and openly taunted the Chinese to take their best shot at him.

Early the following morning, on the deadline of 10 October 1962, 2 Rajputs, leaving Tseng-jong, started off eastward along the ridge toward the bridges that would take them to Yumtso La. Within minutes, Kaul's strategy to liberate Thag La Ridge, Prime Minister Nehru's forward policy and his government's and military's handling of the whole border dispute evaporated. The general recalls the commencement of what would be his worst living nightmare:

The day dawns in this part of the world very early. It was about 0430 hours when I was getting ready and my batman was boiling water for tea. I had hung my mirror on the branch of a tree near my bunker just above Bridge IV and had started shaving when I heard considerable fire from across the river.

A massed battalion of the PLA was rapidly advancing down the Thag La slopes for an assault on Tseng-jong, while heavy mortars bombarded the Indian's hilltop position. Later writing, "Frankly speaking, I had now fully understood all the implications of our predicament … I thought we should reconsider the whole of our position in the theatre," and with his dreams of glory shattered, Kaul transferred command over to Dalvi before setting off for New Delhi to personally brief Nehru. He took Prasad with him. Before his rapid exit from the front, Kaul advised Dalvi to pull his brigade back from the Namka Chu and suspend operations pending clarification and fresh orders from New Delhi.

With sheer determination and tenacity and supported by the machine-gun section above Tseng-jong, the Punjabis repelled the first PLA attack. Knowing he faced overwhelming numbers, the Punjabi commander requested machine-gun and mortar fire from the river line to cover his withdrawal from the untenable position. Dalvi refused, out of concern that, should his main force on Namka Chu become involved in the hitherto limited engagement at Tseng-jong, it would be almost totally wiped out. As it transpired, following Dalvi's order to disengage and retire to the river, the Punjabis withdrew, unhindered by the PLA.

The Punjabis suffered seven killed, eleven wounded and seven missing, while the Chinese admitted to casualties of thirty-three killed and wounded. Out in the open and in full view of the Indians across the river, the Chinese staged a military funeral for the fallen Punjabis.

Arriving in New Delhi on the night of 11 October, Kaul immediately made for the prime minister's residence where Nehru would chair a top-flight meeting. Present were Krishna Menon, cabinet secretaries, the secretaries for external affairs and defence, generals Thapar, Sen and Kaul, commander of the Indian Air Force and senior civil officials.

After briefing the meeting on the battle at Tseng-jong and asked to table his recommendations, Kaul did not push for a withdrawal of 7 Brigade from the south bank of the Namka Chu. Instead, he proposed that India seek immediate and massive military assistance from the United States. Nehru, with some irritation, dismissed the suggestion. However, any consensus reached on what to do next remained unclear; for instance, Cabinet Secretary S. S. Khera stated that Kaul had recommended that he "hold the line of the Namka Chu and hold on to Tsangle". Kaul—rather nebulously—added, "If a chance occurs for us to go across and do something, I will report." While general opinion would suggest that the meeting had agreed to a postponement of Operation Leghorn, no clear instructions emerged. In an indication of frustrated leadership, Nehru left the future of 7 Brigade's disposition with his army chiefs.

The following morning, Thapar and Sen informed Krishna Menon that 7 Brigade would remain on the Namka Chu. Nehru would much later tell parliament that critical decisions had been

taken by Government in full consultation with the Chief of Staff and other senior army officers concerned and in the light of the expert advice. This applies particularly to the decision that the Army should not withdraw in October–November 1962 from its forward position in NEFA.

Many were convinced that Nehru's generals, particularly his close friend Kaul, were merely telling their prime minister what they believed he wanted—and needed—to hear. This was, to a great extent, borne out by the fact that the ambiguous outcome of the meeting at Nehru's residence permeated down to the front in the form of confusion and contradictory orders.

Should Operation Leghorn recommence? Should 7 Brigade be withdrawn from Namka Chu to overwinter in positions where they would be adequately supplied?

Upon his return to Tezpur on 13 October, Kaul informed his staff that New Delhi was adamant that Operation Leghorn had to be executed: nothing had changed.

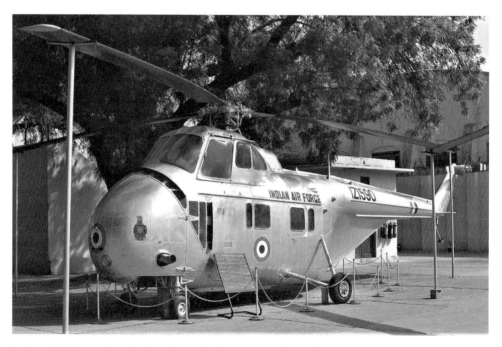

Indian Air Force Sikorsky S-55 (Westland Whirlwind) used extensively in the border-dispute theatres. (Photo Alec Wilson)

Within a few days, however, Thapar signalled Eastern Command requesting an informed assessment of what manpower, ordnance and supplies would be needed to relaunch Operation Leghorn in the spring.

Public opinion demanded restitution and restoration of Indian pride and honour. The Chinese were uninvited guests and had to be forcibly removed from Indian soil at all costs and as soon as possible. On 14 October, Krishna Menon in a public declaration committed his nation's armed forces to an early eviction of the Chinese from Indian territory, including a reference to the western sector: "the policy of the Government of India to eject the Chinese from NEFA, whether it takes one day, a hundred days or a thousand days ... [and to fight the Chinese in Aksai Chin] to the last man, the last gun". This placed those of India's generals who were directly involved in the border operation in an insidious no-win situation: condemned if there was a withdrawal from the Namka Chu river line and condemned if they lost to the Chinese. Few in the Indian military actually believed that victory could be achieved.

Prasad and Dalvi were both fully aware that it would be logistically impossible to maintain the Namka Chu line through the impending winter. Between 12 and 14 October, the 4th Battalion Grenadiers (4 Gren) reached the Namka Chu. They had been deployed from New Delhi, so were not acclimatized to the freezing, mountainous conditions. They arrived exhausted, poorly clothed and ill equipped. A few days later, the battalion's equally ill-prepared—without winter clothing or food—contingent of 450 porters arrived. There were now some 3,000 men on the Indian south bank, 2,500 of them army personnel. There was, however, only winter clothing and tents for 300 at most, which meant that the rest had to suffer in their cotton summer uniforms. Without axes or digging tools, improvised shelters had to be made using parachute material and tree branches.

Thus the tragic farce that Operation Leghorn had become was perpetuated.

The first of the winter's snow fell in the Namka Chu valley on 17 October, making the manual conveyance of a few mortars through the passes a mammoth undertaking. Four artillery pieces from the paratroop unit were parachuted in, but two of the guns sustained such severe damage that they were rendered unserviceable. The gunners themselves had to trek from the Parachute Brigade's base at Agra, coming through the 16,000 feet Karpo La I Pass. The troops were not acclimatized to the high altitude and Arctic conditions, and fatalities resulted. Troops' rations were down to two days and sugar, salt and matches ran out.

Larger supply aircraft were now employed and on a more frequent basis. The Fairchild C-119 'Flying Boxcar', with a cargo capacity of 12,500 kilograms, could ferry in far greater volumes of supplies than the Douglas DC-3 Dakota. However, the air supply was beset with two major problems: one was the speed of the C-119 which made it very difficult for the aircrews to hit very small drop zones; the other was the

Indian troops
recover airdropped
supplies, NEFA, 1962.
(Photo DPR-MOD)

poor quality of the parachutes due to repeated recycling resulting in canopy failure. It was assessed that 7 Brigade only recovered thirty per cent of airdrops, a poor statistic that was compounded by the 3,000-feet, steep incline down which such supplies had to be physically lugged by porters and army pioneers.

On 17 October, Krishna Menon, Sen, Kaul and Dalvi met at Tezpur, where it was made clear that the holding of the position at Tsangle was no longer open to debate: the Gorkhas and Punjabis would remain. Dalvi was ordered to move another company to the position to strengthen the garrison. Many still believe that this sealed 7 Brigade's fate. Supply lines would now be stretched to the limit, and the already flimsy Namka Chu line of defence left weak and irredeemably in jeopardy.

That same day, Kaul developed symptoms of breathing difficulties and a high temperature. Diagnosed by the IV Corps medical officer with a pulmonary infection exacerbated by exhaustion, Kaul was flown to New Delhi the next day for urgent treatment. Upon his arrival in the capital, however, and amidst confusion and contradictory comments between Sen and Kaul, the latter general was not admitted to hospital, but went directly to his house on York Road instead. Here, Kaul retained his command of IV Corps, directing 7 Brigade troop movements from his bedroom.

On the 18th, the already stupefied Dalvi received orders from Kaul to move yet another two companies to Tsangle, another to Bridge IV, and a fourth to patrol the line between Bridge IV and Tsangle. In the face of an imminent PLA assault on the Namka Chu, in utter desperation Dalvi protested. The very next signal to land in

INDIA–CHINA CLASHES ON BORDER

Indian troops, intruding north of the McMahon Line into the Che Dong area of China have intensified their activity all along the Kechilang River [Namka Chu], and attacked Chinese frontier guards at several places in the past 24 hours, the New China news agency reported from Peking today.

The agency said a large number of "fully-armed Indian troops" advanced northward yesterday between points identified as the Hatung Pass and Pangkangting, "apparently ready to cross the river to launch attacks on the Chinese frontier guards there."

Chinese Shelled

During the night the Indians shelled Chinese posts near the Che-Jao bridge, it claimed, and listed other places along the river where the Indians had attacked. The agency attributed the Indian offensive to "important arrangements" made at an emergency meeting, which it said was called last Tuesday by the Indian Prime Minister, Mr. Nehru.

"These events show that the Indian troops, in line with the new arrangements of the Indian authorities are hastening to carry out Nehru's instructions to free China's territory of the Chinese frontier guards."

Coventry Evening Telegraph, Thursday, 18 October 1962

Dalvi's lap was from Prasad: any more dissent would result in his (Dalvi's) field court martial and that of his battalion commanding officers.

Throughout the day, PLA activity on the southern slopes of Thag La escalated. For several days already, labour battalions and hundreds of hardy Tibetan mountain ponies had been ferrying in supplies.

Without taking any precautions to conceal their movements, the first PLA deployments were seen by the Indians on the 19th as 2,000 Chinese troops assembled at Tseng-jong. PLA marking parties were also openly observed preparing the terrain for a night advance. Dalvi immediately contacted Prasad who had now established a 4th Division tactical HQ at Zimithang: the Namka Chu line was in immediate danger of being overrun by the Chinese, so all Indian troops at Tsangle had to be withdrawn to add some strength to 7 Brigade's fragile positions along the river. Prasad, however, remained unmoved: there would be no redeployments. Dalvi had had enough, and he cracked. Speaking from his brigade headquarters a short distance southwest of Dhola Post, the stressed Dalvi informed Prasad that he would resign rather than "stand by and see the troops massacred". Dalvi's ultimatum reached Kaul in New Delhi, having been passed on from IV Corps HQ in Tezpur, where staff refused to assume responsibility for Dalvi's actions. There was, however, no response, and by first light the following morning, the remainder of the Gorkhas prepared to move off Tseng-jong back to Tsangle.

At 5 a.m. on the morning of 20 October 1962, the much-anticipated Chinese assault commenced.

During the night, PLA troops had taken up launch positions, taunting the Indians by lighting fires to keep warm. By this time, the Namka Chu had dropped to fordable levels, making the Indian log bridges useless. Elements of the PLA had waded through the river west of Bridge IV, their passage unhindered as the Indian positions were so spread out that there were yawning gaps in their line. While part of this group had readied themselves for a dawn attack on the Indians' left flank, the rest of the PLA troops had started to scale the ridge toward the 1/9 Gorkhas position on Tsangdhar.

As the 20th dawned, two flares shot into the sky from the massed PLA troops, the signal for artillery and heavy mortars facing the Namka Chu on the Thag La Ridge lower slopes to commence a heavy bombardment of the centre of the Indian line. Dalvi would later recall: "As the first salvoes crashed overhead there were a few minutes of petrifying shock. The contrast with the tranquillity that had obtained hitherto made it doubly impressive. The proximity of the two forces made it seem like an act of treachery."

The PLA in action with a Type 56 (RPD) light machine gun.

Concentrated on the centre of the Indian line, 1/9 Gorkhas and 2 Rajputs took the full brunt of the PLA attack. The Indian positions were quickly penetrated, while elements of 1/9 Gorkhas found themselves exposed and at the mercy of the PLA guns as they moved in the direction of Tsangle. At the same time, 2 Rajputs came under simultaneous attack on both flanks.

The Indians were hopelessly outnumbered and quickly overwhelmed as position after position fell to the savage Chinese assault. Despite scattered gallant acts with the bayonet, by 9 a.m. it was all over for the Gorkhas and Rajputs.

The PLA troops then struck south toward the weakly defended Tsangdhar, where a depleted company of Gorkhas was about to go to the aid of the Indian position on Tsangle. Two paratroop field pieces' crews were annihilated after a desperate but hopeless attempt to stem the Chinese onslaught.

Along the Namka Chu, a now disjointed 7 Brigade was in disarray. Lines of communication had been severed by Chinese artillery, while Rajput and Gorkha signalmen had to abandon their WS No. 31 radio sets for .303 rifles. Albeit that Prasad at 4th Division HQ still felt duty bound to obey orders from the highest level to hold Tsangle at all costs, in the face of impossible odds he capitulated and acquiesced to Dalvi's urgent please to withdraw 7 Brigade HQ to Tsangdhar. Here they might be able to meld with the Gorkhas to make a stand.

The numerical strength and firepower of well-equipped PLA troops made for a rapid realization of the Chinese strategic objective of taking Tsangdhar and Hathung La, and in doing so, encircling the remnants of 7 Brigade on the Namka Chu. On the Indian right flank, the 9th Punjabs and 4 Grenadiers battalions were spared a full assault, the PLA electing to engage the Indian positions at bridges I and II from the other side of the Namka Chu. Fearing yet another humiliating setback, Prasad ordered the two battalions to retire south to Hathung La. However, the PLA arrived at the pass first to block the Indians coming in their direction. At the same time, the leaderless, ragtag dregs of 7 Brigade struck west in full retreat. Cold, hungry and demoralized, the troops staggered through Bhutan and back into India.

Chief of Army Staff General Pran Nath Thapar.

HEAVY FIGHTING IN 2 AREAS ON INDIA'S BORDER

Fighting flared this morning at both ends of the disputed border area between China and India, the New China news agency reported. Both sides blamed each other for starting the fighting.

The Chinese agency said Indian troops, under cover of heavy fire from artillery and machineguns, launched attacks about 3 a.m. in the Chip Chap Valley area of the western sector of India's North-East Frontier, compelling the Chinese border guards to "act resolutely in self-defence." In the eastern sector, the agency said, Indian troops began at 7 a.m. a "large-scale frenzied attack" under cover of fierce shelling, inflicting heavy casualties on Chinese frontier guards in the Kechilang [Namka Chu] River area in the eastern sector.

Menon's Statement
The report of an Indian intrusion In the Chip Chap Valley yesterday and today's reported attack there were the first for several weeks of trouble in the western sector between Sinkiang and the Ladakh region of Kashmir. In New Delhi, Mr. Krishna Menon, the Indian Defence Minister, said Chinese troops launched an attack this morning on Indian posts in the North-East Frontier area and the Ladakh area of Kashmir. Mr Menon. speaking at a Press conference, said the Chinese attack began at 5 a.m. local time on Indian forward posts In the Khinzemane and Dhola areas of the North-East Frontier and the Chip Chap Valley area. Mr Menon also said Indian supply-dropping planes had been attacked in Ladakh and on the North-East Frontier but had successfully returned to base.

"Premeditated"
Mr. Menon said the Chinese were using heavy mortars and machine gun fire and attacked in large numbers. The Chinese attacks were "premeditated and concerted" and heavy fighting was going on. Diplomatic observers in Peking said the tone and speed of transmission of the latest reports reflected the greatest sense of urgency on the Chinese side since the border dispute flared up again early in the summer and since the increase in tension.

Coventry Evening Telegraph, Saturday, 20 October 1962

On 22 October, as Dalvi and a small group of brigade staff were moving cross-country to reach 4th Division HQ, they were captured by Chinese troops: 7 Brigade was no more. At the same time, Prasad was also withdrawing his divisional HQ which was under imminent threat of attack. He arrived at Tawang that evening.

The final scene was one of tragic irony on a battlefield now void of Indian defenders. Tsangle, the strategic position on which New Delhi had placed so much importance for the successful execution of Operation Leghorn, was totally ignored by the PLA. For the Chinese, not only was Tsangle of no tactical value, but their maps—and those of the Indians—showed that the position was in Bhutan. The misguided insistence that Tsangle be defended at all costs resulted directly in the total obliteration of 7 Brigade.

In the frontier's western sector, the PLA simultaneously fell on Indian posts in the disputed Aksai Chin: Chip Chap River valley, the Galwan and in the environs of Pangong Lake. The Galwan post, under PLA siege since August, had come under Chinese artillery fire.

A recent image of the road to Tawang, clearly showing the extremely difficult terrain the troops had to fight in. (Photo Kunal Dalui)

Indian patrol on the Sino-Indian border.

Communications ceased, and the fate of the post remained unknown, but the Indian posts could only display token resistance before being swamped by PLA troops. Western Command ordered the smaller, isolated posts that had not yet been attacked to be abandoned. As in the eastern sector, Nehru's forward policy in Aksai Chin was a dismal and costly failure.

On the morning of 23 October, New Delhi's dailies informed the Indian public of the military disaster at Namka Chu in the North East Frontier Agency. One newspaper declared that "India is at War". Nehru, however, in an attempt to downplay the magnitude of the humiliating defeat his troops had suffered at the hands of superior Chinese forces, informed two visiting opposition MPs that India would maintain diplomatic relations with Beijing. He added that, in no circumstances, would military aid be sought from friendly nations. The public was not unsympathetic toward Nehru, his persona representing the aggrieved nation. But someone had to shoulder the blame, a scapegoat had to be found and made to pay.

Three days after the Chinese attack, a group of thirty MPs of the ruling Indian National Congress (generally referred to as Congress) determined that the government, parliament and Nehru had been grossly misled by defence minister Krishna Menon. Within days, opposition MPs joined the lynch mob calling for the hapless minister's head. The added weight of the chief ministers of the Indian states decided the issue as, on 31 October, Nehru assumed personal control of the defence portfolio. Krishna Menon was sidelined to the newly formed Ministry for Defence Production. Nehru went on to install the chief minister of the state of Maharashtra as defence minister.

In the international arena and, as was expected, the West, led by Britain and the United States, came out in solid support of the Indian cause. In a letter to Nehru, U.S. President John F. Kennedy said: "Our sympathy in the situation is wholeheartedly with you. You have displayed an impressive degree of forbearance and patience in dealing with the Chinese." Washington recognized the McMahon Line as the *de jure* international border between India and China. Of significance, was the U.S. offer of material aid. London followed suit, expressing solidarity with India by also offering assistance.

Unsurprisingly, the African- and Arab-dominated bloc of non-aligned nations remained silent, with the exception of the former British colony of Ghana, whose first independent head of government, Kwame Nkrumah, strongly criticized British Prime Minister Harold Macmillan for choosing sides in the Sino-Indian conflict. What was unexpected, however, was Moscow's stance.

Despite the Sino-Soviet rift caused by divergent ideologies, Soviet leader Nikita Khrushchev dispatched a letter to Nehru as early as 20 October, the day the Chinese launched their attack, cautioning Nehru that, by taking up arms against the Chinese to resolve the border dispute was "a very dangerous path". Within days, on the 24th, Beijing proposed an immediate cessation of hostilities along its shared frontier with India, which would be followed by peace talks. The next day, *Pravda,*

Nehru at NEFA, 1962. The heavy winter wear of these troops is an indication of the extremely cold Himalayan border areas.

the mass-circulation broadsheet of the Communist Party of the Soviet Union, printed an unreserved pro-China and anti-West editorial, pointing the finger of blame directly at "British colonialists". Moscow now vacillated on the question of supplying the Indian Air Force with MiG fighter jets.

But it was a superpower standoff on the other side of the globe that was the main cause of Moscow's sudden sympathy to its Chinese comrades. On 14 October, U.S. intelligence discovered the presence of Soviet ballistic missiles on Cuban soil and within striking distance of the U.S. mainland. As the situation deteriorated and the U.S. placed a shipping embargo around Fidel Castro's Caribbean island nation, Cold War tensions threatened to catapult the world into a third international conflagration. In such a situation of extreme danger, Moscow could ill afford to be at odds with China. However, what became known as the Cuban Missile Crisis fizzled out on 28 October when Khrushchev stepped back and agreed to withdraw his missiles from Cuba.

Both sides would blame the other. (*Coventry Evening Telegraph*, Monday, 22 October 1962)

The PLA employed Type 59 130mm towed field guns, a licensed-built copy of the Soviet M-46 shown here at a Russian museum. (Photo Mike 1979 Russia)

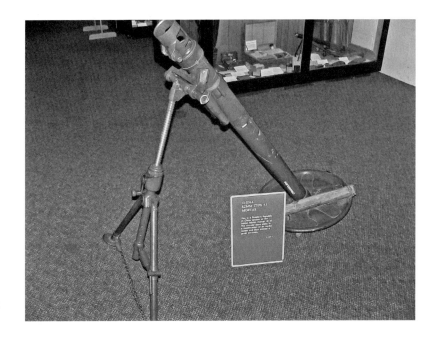

Chinese 82mm Type 53 mortar. (Photo Mark Pellegrini)

Assam Rifles
cap badge and shoulder title

9 Gorkha Rifles shoulder title

Indian Artillery
cap badge

Rajput shoulder title

Garhwal Rifles shoulder title

Punjab Regt shoulder title

Indian Engineers   Indian Signals Corps
cap badge   cap badge

Kumaon Regt shoulder title

Ordnance Corps shoulder title

India Tibet Border Police
shoulder title

Badges and shoulder titles of Indian Army regiments that saw active service in the border conflict. (Courtesy Colonel Dudley Wall collection)

5. WALONG TO BOMDI LA

At Army HQ in the Indian capital, Chief of Army Staff General Thapar was in a state of flux. With the disintegration of 7 Brigade and the fall of the Namka Chu line, combined with the uncertainty of immediate PLA objectives, Thapar impulsively determined that the Indian garrison at Tawang should not be taken by the Chinese.

On 22 October, Eastern Command chief, Lieutenant-General Sen, flew into Tawang by helicopter. Here, he left the commanding officers of the 1st Sikh Battalion and the 4th Battalion Garhwal Rifles in no doubt that Tawang had to be held, regardless of the cost. The general offered a semblance of hope by promising that two infantry brigades would be deployed to assist with the defence of the Tawang garrison. Sen returned to Tezpur the next day.

By now, the PLA force that had decimated 7 Brigade, was striking southeast in a three-pronged manoeuvre. Estimated to be at three-regiment strength, the western prong halted ten miles from Tawang on the 23rd, where they were joined by the central prong that had marched via Khinzemane and along the Nyamjang Chu River. Later that day, the eastern prong crossed the McMahon Line at Bum La Pass, striking directly south along the old trade route to Tawang.

At Army HQ, Director of Military Operations (DMO), Brigadier D. K. Palit, conveyed to Thapar his misgivings about the wisdom of trying to defend Tawang against such insurmountable odds. Thapar turned to Nehru to assist with the strategic dilemma in which he now found himself fully embroiled. However, the Indian premier simply responded by telling his chief of army staff that Tawang was a military situation requiring military decisions. At IV Corps HQ in Tezpur, Brigadier-General Staff K. K. Singh was simultaneously urging Sen to evacuate Tawang. On the day that the Chinese commenced their operations, at his house in New Delhi General Kaul had been instructed to cease any communication with NEFA and to relinquish command of IV Corps.

On 23 October, a signal went out from IV Corps to Tawang, ordering the evacuation of the garrison and withdrawal sixty miles down the road to Bomdi La Pass. It was believed that this would facilitate a quicker build-up of Indian forces to block the PLA. But in yet another confusing contradiction, DMO Palit was pushing for the Indian forces to consolidate at Se La Pass, a gap in the mountains that he believed would offer their retreating forces a perfectly defensible position against the advancing Chinese. Faced with an opportunity to reverse fortunes and restore India's faith in its military to defend the homeland from foreign invasion, on the 23rd Sen issued

Indian troops having to physically haul an army supply truck up a virtually impassable 'road' in NEFA, 1962.

a countermand ordering the troops to only fall back as far as Se La. He deflected protests from his field commanders by telling them that he was merely complying with the wishes of cabinet, and therefore government. The decision, apart from confirming the divisiveness that had permeated the Indian Army's command structure at this time of crisis, would be fatal.

Se La was not impregnable. Flanked by 1,000-feet-high peaks, the 14,600-feet pass had rough-hewn tracks circumventing it. The extremely steep road from Tawang rose 5,000 feet to Se La and, at best, could only accommodate one-ton trucks in a debilitating journey that took several days. Reinforcements would have to come from units on the plains below, but they would not be acclimatized and would suffer in the rarified air. The magnitude of defending Se La increased significantly with the added need to keep the road to Bomdi La clear of Chinese troops who would almost certainly cut off access to Se La. This entailed securing sixty miles of treacherous, high-altitude road through broken terrain.

Air supply would also be problematic as potential drop zones were few and very small. Air support was also ruled out, for fear of Chinese retaliation that could include the bombing of Indian cities such as Calcutta.

On 23 October, hundreds of civilians and Buddhist lamas from the monastery joined the Indian troop withdrawal from Tawang. The two Tawang battalions—1 Sikh and 4 Garhwal—took up positions on the south bank of the Jang River. Two days after the Indian evacuation of Tawang, the PLA walked into the position without

CHINESE TAKE TAWANG IN MAJOR VICTORY

Chinese troops have taken the Indian administrative centre of Tawang, on the North-east Frontier, and won control of the upper reaches of the Namyahng river valley, running south through Bhutan to the Indian plains, it was announced in New Delhi yesterday.

There is speculation in Delhi that the Chinese might pause after taking Tawang to re-form and make new peace overtures to India. India, however, is now adamant that no talks can be held unless the Chinese withdraw behind the line they held before the present fighting began.

Monastery Prayers
At Tawang, 600 shaven-headed monks had lit butter-oil lamps and planted prayer flags in ritual prayers for the protection of their monastery. The monks feared that the Chinese would inflict punishment on the monastery for the warm welcome and hospitality it gave to the Dalai Lama in April 1959, when he fled from Tibet to India.

Mr. Nehru, the Indian Prime Minister, appealed to the Indian people yesterday to follow the British example after Dunkirk and rally to defeat the "massive invasion of India by China". The Chinese had deployed nearly 30,000 troops along the Himalayas, he said, and had shocked India out of an "artificial atmosphere of her own creation". India had been "out touch with reality". Russia yesterday declared itself in favour of a negotiated settlement of the dispute between India and China. It supported China's call for talks, but carefully avoided taking sides in the dispute.

Birmingham Daily Post, Friday, 26 October 1962

firing a single shot. To the east, by 24/25 October, units of the PLA had advanced south through Tulung La Pass, conducting exploratory strikes in the direction of Walong.

In the western sector, the Chinese also continued with their operations in Aksai Chin. After encountering extremely strong resistance from Gorkha troops to the north of Pangong Lake, on 21 October the PLA neutralized these Indian posts. A week later, the posts in the Demchok vicinity were also overrun. Other posts, such as Daulet Beg Oldi, were evacuated under orders from Western Command before the PLA could strike. All the while, the Western Command's General Officer Commanding-in-Chief General Daulet Singh was assiduously and with some haste augmenting Indian troop

Elements of the Indian Army struggle with heavy loads, Walong sector, NEFA, 1962. (Photo DPR-MOD)

strengths along the front by transferring troops from Kashmir. The command's transport capabilities were concentrated to provide maximum logistical support to the strengthening of the Ladakh front. The successful management of operations in the western sector meant that by the beginning of November, a divisional headquarters had been set up at Leh, in addition to an infantry brigade of four battalions. By the 17th, another brigade arrived at the Leh garrison.

Back in the eastern sector, prevailing levels of indecision saw the replacement of several senior commanders in the theatre. On 24 October, Lieutenant-General Harbaksh Singh arrived from Simla to assume command of IV Corps. Prasad was relieved as commander of 4th Division and replaced with the commandant of the National Cadet Corps in New Delhi, Major-General A. S. Pathania. The commanders of 62, 65 and 5 brigades were also replaced. In similar fashion, army units were also being shuffled about, until the situation arose in NEFA where not a single brigade retained its original formation battalions.

A landmark event in the progress of the Sino-Indian conflict took place in New Delhi on 29 October when Nehru informed the U.S. ambassador that he accepted

Washington's offer to assist with any of India's military needs during the crisis. Shedding his mantle of non-alignment, Nehru and his cabinet had to face the reality that India could not withstand the Chinese onslaught without the volume and sophistication of war matériel that the U.S. was in a position to supply. The U.S. embassy was handed an inventory that had already been prepared, although it proved a challenge to the Americans to interpret. Five days later, the first American aid arrived in India, ferried by modern, large cargo aircraft from U.S. bases in West Germany. In Beijing, the *People's Daily* accused the Indian leader of being a "sell-out to U.S. imperialism".

However, what this meant for the Chinese and already expressed by some in the corridors of power in Beijing, was that with U.S. entrepreneurs now in the game, the supply of matériel to New Delhi would "probably go on for ever". Further confidence and comfort for India in the conflict came soon after the Cuban missile crisis had ended. Early in November, the Soviet reverted to appealing to both antagonists for a ceasefire and peace talks.

Beijing resuscitated the Sino-Soviet rift by accusing Khrushchev of adventurism in the Caribbean, worsened by buckling under pressure from the Kennedy administration and removing his missiles from Cuba. China boasted that their successful conduct and completion of the Indian border campaign would prove that imperialist

Soviet leader Nikita Khrushchev (centre), with Cuban revolutionary Fidel Castro over his left shoulder.

intimidation and the ineptitude of Khrushchev and his "revisionist clique" would be ignored as innocuous.

After the Namka Chu rout, in the eastern sector there was a lull in the fighting, accompanied by a parallel reduction in the Indians' urgency to reinforce Se La, Bomdi La and the road connecting the two garrisons. Of the three Punjab divisions ultimately moved into NEFA, two only arrived after the ceasefire. From the remaining division, only one of its brigades would see any action. The division in Nagaland, initially on standby, was stood down during this period of false peace. However, what was very evident to the forward Indian positions was that the Chinese were working round the clock to construct a road along the old trade route from Bum La on the McMahon Line to Tawang. In early November, Indian Air Force reconnaissance sorties detected the movement of PLA heavy vehicles in Tawang, confirming that the road had been completed. Work then immediately commenced on the road to Se La.

After only four days at the helm of IV Corps, Harbaksh Singh was replaced by the previous incumbent, General Kaul who, All-India Radio claimed had fully recovered from the "chill and severe attack of bronchitis which he had contracted in the front line". Controversy continued to infest the move, with the military stating that it was the government's choice. "Now God help us!" was reputedly to have been said by an officer at 4th Division HQ when the news came out. On 29 October, Kaul resumed command of IV Corps. Harbaksh Singh was given the command of XXXIII Corps, and Umrao Singh transferred to a staff job at Army HQ in New Delhi.

Situated in what is now the Indian state of Arunachal Pradesh (formerly NEFA), Walong is India's easternmost town. Sitting on the west bank of the Lohit River (a tributary of the Brahmaputra), it is about twelve miles south of the Chinese border and the Tibetan trading town of Rima.

At first, the Walong operational sector fell under 4th Division's 5 Infantry Brigade. After the loss of Tawang to the PLA, New Delhi made the decision to establish a new divisional headquarters, exclusive of the Se La–Bomdi La sector that would remain with the 4th Division. Designated 2nd Infantry Division, the command was given to Major-General M. S. Pathania, cousin to the 4th Division commander, A. S. Pathania. The assignment of 181 Infantry Brigade, however, did not sit at all well with M. S. Pathania. At the general's insistence, he was given 11 Infantry Brigade instead, a fateful move for the brigade that was deployed to the Walong sector. A while later, a Gorkha battalion was moved to Walong, and then back to the plains before being sent to Walong a second time.

By the start of November, 2nd Division's HQ was firmly established. At Walong, the Indian garrison comprised three infantry battalions of 11 Brigade and elements of the Assam Rifles. A confident M. S. Pathania approached IV Corps for one more battalion to augment his Walong force, certain that he could then drive the PLA back

Indian troops crossing a river in Lohit, Walong sector, 1962. (Photo DPR-MOD)

across the McMahon Line. Corps HQ, however, turned the request down, based on an assessment that the PLA was only at division strength in Rima. On 11 November, M. S. Pathania received division's refusal, but this information was not passed on to 11 Brigade. Indian preparations for an attack on the PLA continued, with the 13th scheduled for the launch of the assault. It was envisaged that the operation would be successfully completed the following day, 14 November, Nehru's birthday. The brigade's victory would provide the Indian premier with the perfect birthday gift.

On the 14th, 11 Brigade launched its attack on the PLA position, believed to be at company strength. With artillery and heavy mortars in support, two companies of the 6th Kumaon Battalion, already weary from constant patrolling, the rugged troops from one of India's most decorated regiment engaged the PLA bunkers for nearly six hours, before they stalled about fifty yards from the crest of the ridge with withering Chinese fire and exhaustion taking its toll. During the night, the PLA left their defensive positions and cleared the surviving Kumaonis from the hill: fewer than half of the Indians made it back to base.*

---

* The battalion celebrates 14 November as Walong Day.

The PLA continued to pour down the slopes, smashing into the Indian defences. Having expended all their ammunition in support of the earlier Kumaoni attack, the Indian artillery stood silent as the main PLA force struck at dawn on 16 November.

The Indians tenaciously fought on against impossible odds, and at some posts not a single soldier survived. At this time, the total annihilation of 11 Brigade was imminent, forcing Kaul to order an immediate withdrawal at around 10 a.m. Unfortunately, the order did not reach all the Indian positions, so the troops were left behind to fight on until they either ran out of ammunition and were taken prisoner or were killed.

Kaul and M. S. Pathania flew out of Walong in the second-last flight in a de Havilland Canada DHC-3 Otter, a short take-off and landing aircraft. At Teju, Kaul dispatched a lengthy signal on the Walong débâcle to Army HQ, concluding:

> It is now my duty to urge that the enemy thrust is now so great and his overall strength is so superior that you should ask the highest authorities to get such foreign armed forces to come to our aid as are willing to do so without which, as I have said before and which I reiterate, it seems beyond the capacity of our armed forces to stem the tide of the superior Chinese forces which he has and will continue to concentrate against us to our disadvantage. This is not a counsel of fear, but facing stark realities.

The cohesionless remnants of 11 Brigade trickled down the Lohit valley toward the plains below. However, the dazed survivors faced a bottleneck at the 300-feet-deep Lohit River gorge. Only a single, rope suspension bridge was available as an escape route, unlike their assailants who had crossed the Lohit in rubber inflatables. Those Indians trapped on the eastern side of the gorge sustained heavy losses through both Chinese gunfire and deprivation.

Meanwhile, the situation in the western sector bore little resemblance to the tragedies that continued to unfold in NEFA. Western Command aggressively pushed ahead with the transfer of border troops from Kashmir to Ladakh. By the end of the first week in October, construction of the road from Leh southeast to Chusul had been completed.

A fortnight later, 14,000-feet Chushul was established as a brigade headquarters. The only remaining Indian defence post that fell within Chinese-claimed territory was just to the east of Chushul. The village itself, with its airstrip, fell outside the disputed line. Unlike their brothers-in-arms in the eastern sector, in Ladakh the military did not risk its troops with deployments to questionable forward 'tactical' positions.

Toward the end of October, five Indian Air Force Soviet-made Antonov An-12 (NATO designated 'Cub') transports delivered five French-made AMX-13 light tanks to the brigade at Chushul.

INDIANS YIELD GROUND TO ASSAULTS BY CHINESE

But Hold on Another Front
Indian troops today yielded some ground before massive Chinese attacks at Walong, but repulsed Communist assaults at another point on the Himalayan front, a Defence Ministry spokesman said in New Delhi today. This was after reports of a "major reverse" for the Chinese—their first since the fighting approached the strategic village of Walong. Fierce fighting is continuing on the North-East Frontier, with heavy casualties on both the Indian and Chinese sides, the spokesman said.

Four Chinese attacks "in substantial strength" were repulsed around Jang, 300 miles west of Walong. Jang is near Tawang and below the Indian defence line. The rest of the battle-line was reported quiet. The spokesman said that the Chinese attacked at Walong in "Numbers considerably superior to ours," after artillery and heavy mortar fire.

Given Up
"Our troops are offering stout resistance but had to yield after successive attacks by the enemy," he said. Fierce fighting was still going on according to the last report. The spokesman said Indian troops had had to give up the forward slopes of the Chinese hill position near Walong, which they had regained two days ago. Replying to questions, he said there was an airstrip south of Walong and he hoped it was still in Indian hands. The fighting had been North and North-West of Walong.

In contrast to the Walong threat Chinese attacks at Jang appeared to be only another—although stronger—in a series of raids back and faith in the no-man's-land there.

Asked if the Indians had taken any prisoners in the fighting so far, the Defence Ministry spokesman replied: "Nil."

The Indian Red Cross Society today confirmed that the Chinese have notified it that they hold 927 prisoners of war.

Coventry Evening Telegraph, Saturday, 17 November 1962

On 17 November, large numbers of PLA troops were seen advancing toward the Indian line, and in the early hours of the 18th, the Chinese commenced laying down a heavy artillery barrage on Indian positions in the valley and on the Chushul airfield.

Indian dugout, Ladakh, western sector.

The French-built AMX-13 light tank. (Photo The Bern Files)

As day dawned, the PLA employed heavy mortars and recoilless guns to soften the outlying Indian defences that were barely scrapes in the frozen ground. Individual Indian positions were enveloped or outflanked and eradicated.

In what became known as the battle of Rezang La, virtually a whole company of Indian troops perished while fighting or froze to death. 'Charlie' Company of the 13th Kumaon Battalion, comprising 120 *jawan** faced a savage onslaught from an estimated 5,000 PLA troops supported by artillery on the morning of 18 November. Commanded by Major Shaitan Singh, the Indians put up a remarkable fight, accounting for almost 1,300 Chinese troops.

Isolated from the rest of their battalion in the broken terrain, five platoons of Kumaonis held the Rezang La Pass southeast of the Chushul valley. As the PLA attacked Nos. 7 and 8 platoons, the Indians fought back with Bren light machine guns, 3-inch mortars, grenades and .303 rifles, inflicting significant casualties among the Chinese. In another unsuccessful frontal assault, some 350 PLA troops were repelled by No. 9 Platoon, again sustaining major losses. Enveloping the Indian position, an estimated 400 PLA troops attacked from the rear, employing machine guns, heavy artillery and mortars. A company-strength PLA unit simultaneously charged No. 7 Platoon but were beaten off by the Kumaonis firing 3-inch mortars.

Displaying gallant leadership and placing his life before those of his men, in the heat of the battle Major Shaitan Singh moved tirelessly from one position of Kumaonis to the next, cajoling and encouraging his men. On one such dash, he was felled by medium machine-gun fire and fatally wounded. It is said that Singh was moved by one of his soldiers to a place of relative safety between two boulders, where he succumbed to his wounds.

Only eight members of the company survived: three wounded found their way back to battalion HQ and five were taken prisoner by the PLA. In February 1963, a recovery party found the frozen bodies of 114 Kumaonis and that of company commander Major Singh at Rezang La. Many were still holding their rifles. The PLA had only removed the bodies of their own dead.

Major Shaitan Singh was posthumously awarded the Param Vir Chakra (PVC), India's highest military decoration, equivalent to the Victoria Cross, for his 'most conspicuous bravery in the presence of the enemy'. There were also five recipients of the Vir Chakra (VrC) gallantry award made for 'acts of bravery in the battlefield', and four of the Sena Medal (SM), awarded for 'such individual acts of exceptional devotion to duty or courage as have special significance for the Army'.

---

* all other ranks below commissioned officer

After five hours of intense and desperate fighting, the PLA had neutralized all the Indian hill positions. The Indians consolidated on high ground overlooking brigade HQ, expecting to face another head-on PLA assault. However, the Chinese did not push home their offensive, stopping at their claim line that did not include Chusul itself.

Meanwhile to the east in NEFA, by 17 November 4th Division had been bolstered to ten infantry battalions, supported by reasonable quantities of artillery, heavy mortars and a few light tanks. The division would have been a force to reckon with, had it not been for the fact that it was spread over three positions along a sixty-mile stretch of a treacherous route that was a road in name only.

At Se La, Brigadier Hoshiar Singh commanded 62 Brigade, comprising five infantry battalions. The garrison relied on being supplied by air and road, but the extremely slow rate at which replenishments came through meant that at any given point in time, the brigade only ever had a day's worth of supplies. The garrison therefore remained short of ammunition and other matériel essential for their defence.

To the southeast, on the road to Bomdi La, divisional HQ was based at Dirang Dzong, together with 65 Brigade and two infantry battalions. Lying in a valley, the garrison had

Se La Pass. (Photo Saurabhgupta8)

few defensive advantages, yet little was done to fortify the position. Hut and tented accommodation was in the open, virtually unprotected by any earthen embankments.

At the southern end of the sector, 48 Brigade, under Brigadier Gurbax Singh and consisting of three infantry battalions, was garrisoned at Bomdi La. Three commanding hills dominated Bomdi La, yielding the potential for a very strong defensive position had there been sufficient troops at this pass. Whilst division was satisfied that the Se La–Bomdi La was as secure as they could achieve under difficult circumstances, there remained a critical imponderable: the Bailey Trail.

In 1913, the Indian-born Frederick Marshman Bailey, a British intelligence officer with the rank of captain, accompanied by Captain Henry Morshead from the Survey of India, embarked on an unauthorized expedition to follow the course of the Yarlung Tsangpo River, an upper tributary of the Brahmaputra River, from Tibet all the way to the Indian Ocean. Starting at the massive Tsangpo gorges in the Himalaya, the party trekked south into what would become NEFA. Crossing the mountain crest at Tulung La Pass, they then journeyed through the 15,600-feet Tse La Pass, and on to Poshing La at 14,000 feet. Continuing directly south, Bailey and Morshead arrived at Thembang, a small hamlet situated on a spur overlooking the Se La–Bomdi La valley.

General A. S. Pathania took cognizance of Bailey's Trail, but only to minimize its importance in the belief that PLA troops, especially in winter, would not be able to use the trail in numbers of any consequence. If elements of the PLA were able to reach the road and set up a roadblock, Pathania was confident that Indian troops from either Dirang Dzong or Bomdi La would be able to remove the Chinese presence. Since early November, Pathania had been deploying small units of troops to positions that he assessed would serve to block any potential PLA flanking moves. From the Bomdi La garrison, a company was moved to Phutang, south of Dirang Dzong, and on 12 November, a platoon from the 5th Guards Battalion (5 Guards) was moved to bolster the Assam Rifles at Poshing La. The next day, a further two Guards platoons were deployed to the garrison, bringing the Guards up to company strength.

Toward the end of the day on the 15th, a signal was passed on to 4th Division HQ reporting that forward elements of Indian troops had been eradicated by PLA troops of battalion strength. Attaching little credibility to the alleged size of the PLA force, Pathania issued orders for another company of 5 Guards to be sent up the Bailey Trail to rid it of PLA troops. As it transpired, on the 16th, the balance of 5 Guards left Bomdi La in the direction of Poshing La. They left behind a much-depleted garrison of six companies, representing a mere thirty per cent of the troops required to adequately defend it.

Marching through the night, 5 Guards arrived at Thembang early the following morning, where they promptly began to dig in as best they could. Around early afternoon, an estimated 1,500 PLA troops launched an attack on the Indian position. After three hours of engagement with the Chinese, during which the Indians inflicted heavy casualties, the Guards started to run out of ammunition. Hearing of the imminent demise of the Guards, 48 Brigade HQ at Bomdi La granted the Indian troops permission to retire. As the light faded and in dense jungle, any remaining semblance of a controlled fighting unit evaporated and the troops bombshelled. Not a single soldier would find his way back to Bomdi La, and it was several weeks later before the remnants of 5 Guards staggered onto the plains. The PLA had now successfully gained a section of the road between Bomdi La and Dirang Dzong.

Several miles to the north of Se La, at dawn on the morning of the 17th the 4 Garhwal holding position came under a sustained PLA attack. By late afternoon, the Garhwals had fought off five attempts by the Chinese troops to neutralize their position.

At 62 Brigade HQ, Hoshiar Singh pulled the Garhwals back to underpin the defences at Se La Pass. Now with five interlinked infantry battalions and several field guns, and while the inflow of supplies remained constant, the Indians had established a substantial defensive position. However, realizing that there was an increasing danger of his divisional headquarters at Dirang Dzong being outflanked on both sides, Pathania sought permission from IV Corps at Tezpur to relocate southward. However, Kaul was still out in a helicopter assessing the situation south of

Indian artillery piece, NEFA, 1962.

Walong, with the result that no one at corps HQ was prepared to accede to Pathania's appeal.

Pathania's strategies now drifted to the imperative of a strong stand at Bomdi La. This would entail 62 Brigade relinquishing Se La before marching to divisional HQ at Dirang Dzong. Here they would merge with 65 Brigade, then strike toward Bomdi La, eliminating the PLA roadblock in the process. The Indians would then have an extremely strong garrison at Bomdi La, comprising three infantry brigades. This had in fact been what senior IV Corps officers had been pushing for from the start, but the build-up of PLA forces in the sector up to 17 November meant that the Indians had missed this window of opportunity to consolidate its troops in one position. Now, 4th Division could either elect to make a fighting stand at Dirang Dzong, or run the gauntlet of an unstructured dash for Bomdi La.

By this time Chief of Army Staff Thapar and the commander of Eastern Command, Sen, had arrived at Tezpur, but Kaul had not yet returned from his field visits. In spite of their superior rank to Kaul, they too refused to give Pathania any decision to his request of an evacuation to Bomdi La: he would have to await the return of Kaul.

Kaul arrived back at Tezpur at 7 p.m. of the night of 17 November to the news that PLA forces were about to envelope the Se La garrison. Being made aware of Pathania's plight, Kaul, Thapar, Sen and DMO Brigadier Palit went into private conference, the rest of the staff officers excluded from the meeting. Thirty minutes later a consensus had been reached and the decision made to evacuate the garrisons at both Se La and Dirang Dzong and retire to Bomdi La.

Technical difficulties meant that the signal to 4th Division was delayed, during which time Palit planted doubt over their decision to withdraw by pointing out that they would incur the wrath of the Indian people if they discovered that 12,000 of their troops had shied away from defending the nation from the Chinese invaders.

Helmet Top Walong Memorial, Arunachal Pradesh.

The signal was cancelled and replaced with a fresh one drawn up by Kaul with assistance from Thapar and Sen:

1. You will hold on to your present positions to the best of your ability. When any position becomes untenable I delegate the authority to you to withdraw to any alternative position you can hold.
2. Approximately 400 enemy have already cut the road Bomdi La–Dirang Dzong. I have ordered Commander 48 Brigade to attack this enemy force tonight speedily and resolutely and keep this road clear at all costs. You may be cut off by the enemy at Senge Dzong, Dirang and Bomdi La.
3. 67 Infantry Brigade less one battalion will reach Bomdi La by morning 18th November. Use your tanks and other arms to the fullest extent to clear lines of communication.

There can be little doubt that Pathania had been landed with the full burden of critical tactical decision-making. The consequential fallout of his actions would rest entirely and only with him.

The instruction to 48 Brigade to clear the PLA roadblock elicited resistance from brigade commander Brigadier Gurbax Singh: with only six companies at his disposal, such a task would be impossible without significantly compromising the integrity of the Bomdi La defences. Heeding the brigade commander's concerns, Kaul deferred the order until the next morning when two infantry battalions were to arrive at Bomdi La.

That night, fatal confusion arose between divisional HQ at Dirang Dzong and 62 Brigade at Se La. One of Hoshiar Singh's battalions, in a key defensive position, was ordered to fall back, but was this a redeployment to augment the garrison at Se La, or was it the commencement of the anticipated and requested withdrawal? Pathania would argue that it was only a consolidatory redeployment, while Hoshiar Singh understood it as the start of a staggered withdrawal. Shortly after midnight, the forward battalion fell back, passing through the other two battalions at Se La. The waiting PLA troops quietly took over the positions the Indians had just vacated.

The PLA opened fire on one of the two remaining 62 Brigade battalions. As the Indians fell back under withering fire, the Chinese penetrated Se La. Daybreak on the 18th saw 62 Brigade fleeing Se La, in their haste abandoning field guns, heavy mortars, supplies and unopened crates of American-made automatic assault rifles. As reports came through of 62 Brigade's withdrawal—telephone lines were still operational—Pathania learned that PLA troops had already appeared on the road south of Se La, threatening the brigade's retreat.

A short while later, the commander of a company sent to cover one of the approaches to Dirang Dzong arrived in an agitated state with the news that PLA troops had just attacked his men. Within minutes of his arrival, elements of the PLA opened up on the divisional headquarters with small-arms fire.

Pathania, having exhausted all his options, ordered the evacuation—4th Division HQ and 65 Brigade—of Dirang Dzong. Selecting a few of his staff officers and accompanied by a handful of troops, Pathania left his HQ at around 7 a.m. on the 18th, trekking south to Phutang. There he was to pick up a company of Indian troops before striking east to Bomdi La. However, upon his arrival at Phutang, he received news that Bomdi La had fallen to the PLA, so he moved off southward to the plains instead.

At Dirang Dzong it was each man for himself, as a leaderless amalgam of two infantry battalions, an artillery crew, a light-tank squadron and a miscellany of several hundred headquarters staff sought avenues of escape. One of the battalions succeeded in reaching the plains, while PLA ambushes, rugged terrain and freezing winter took their toll on the amorphous Indian column struggling to reach Bomdi La. Over the next few days, groups of Indian troops were killed or taken prisoner. On 27 November, Brigadier Hoshiar was shot and killed at Phutang.

By the morning of the 18th, the garrison at Bomdi La, although severely weakened to only six companies, was waiting for the Chinese in established defensive positions, supported by artillery, four light tanks and heavy mortars. At 11 a.m., Kaul ordered 48 Brigade commander Gurbax Singh, despite his vehement protestations,

Indian troops on the move, NEFA.

to immediately dispatch a mobile column of infantry and supporting armour and artillery toward Dirang Dzong to clear the road of PLA forces. Personnel from administration, services and engineers were armed and formed into platoons to plug some of the gaps created in the defences by the mobile column.

Ten minutes after the column had left, the PLA mounted an attack, but the Indian defences held. Infantry from the column were immediately ordered to return, but as they approached their previous positions on the Bomdi La perimeter, they discovered that the Chinese had already taken occupancy. As the PLA launched a second, much larger attack, the infantry found themselves full

---

INDIA AIRLIFT FOR BRITONS IN PERIL

From Kamal Sharma, New Delhi, Monday

British women and children were tonight being airlifted to safety from the path of the Red Chinese avalanche in India. This was the news at the end of the darkest day for India since the Communists surged across the Himalayas a month ago. The British women and children in peril are the families of tea planters and oil men who live in the Assam plains—and the Chinese were less than thirty miles away tonight.

First families to leave are those living north of the broad Brahmaputra River, a British spokesman said in New Delhi.

Thrust

They are being brought out, he said, "not because of any panic but because they would be in the way". The number being evacuated was not stated but it is known that about 1,500 British men, women and children live in the Assam plains. It was not stated whether the RAF or the Indian Air Force was carrying out the airlift.

The Chinese on the threshold of Assam—the tea exports of which are India's biggest foreign exchange-earner—have thrust forty miles beyond Bomdila [Bomdi La]. This key administrative town—from which a good road runs downhill to the Assam plains—was captured today. Its population of 2,000 were evacuated in time, Indian Premier Nehru told the nation in a broadcast.

Daily Mirror, Tuesday, 20 November 1962

---

exposed. The Chinese quickly overran several weak Indian positions before directing fire on brigade HQ. The Indian field guns and tanks briefly held the Chinese back while troops mounted a counterattack. But by 4 p.m., it was clear that the situation was hopeless, forcing Gurbax Singh to order a withdrawal eight miles south to Rupa.

However, the brigade commander found that the two infantry battalions that he had banked on being at Rupa had not arrived. One of the battalions had come up via a different route and entered Bomdi La. Under cover of darkness, Gurbax Singh retrieved the troops, unchallenged by the PLA. On the night of the 18th, while establishing defence emplacements around Rupa, Gurbax Singh received a signal from IV Corps HQ to pull back to the village of Foothills just above the plains. As the Indians started to move out, Kaul, at this time in Foothills, ordered 48 Brigade to make a stand at Rupa. As the Indians retraced their steps, they came under heavy fire from PLA forces already ensconced in the hills overlooking Rupa. The defence of Rupa no longer possible, IV Corps ordered the brigade to fall back to Chaku where it would stand a better chance of stemming the Chinese advance any farther south. The brigade arrived at Chaku after nightfall on the 19th.

Casualty evacuation by Sikorsky helicopter.

Soon after midnight, PLA troops conducted a three-pronged attack on Chaku, resulting in the ultimate disintegration of 48 Brigade as a combat unit. Small, disparate groups, constituting the remnants of the brigade, made their way to the plains. As of 3 a.m, on 20 November, NEFA was void of any organized Indian military formations. Fearing that the PLA was about to march onto the plains, Kaul move his HQ almost a hundred miles west to Gauhati, situated on the opposite side of the Brahmaputra.

While Nehru in a public broadcast lamented that the string of defeats was "very serious and saddening to us" in his diary entry for 20 November, the American ambassador to India wrote: "It was the day of ultimate panic in Delhi, the first time I have ever witnessed the disintegration of public morale."

The Indian Army was at a distinct disadvantage against the Chinese during the war. Units were equipped with pre-independence British and Commonwealth Second World War-vintage weaponry, such as the .303 bolt-action rifle and 3-inch mortar shown here being used by British troops in the Italian campaign.

Major Shaitan Singh PVC, officer commanding C Company, 13th Battalion,
Kumaon Regiment, died with 114 of his
men while attempting to hold Rezang
La in the Chusul sector against superior
Chinese forces on 18 November 1962.
Singh was posthumously awarded the
Param Vir Chakra (PVC), India's highest
military decoration, for "supreme
courage, leadership and exemplary
devotion to duty" while himself
severely wounded.

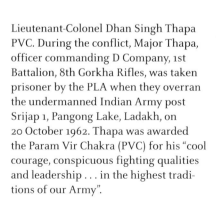

Lieutenant-Colonel Dhan Singh Thapa
PVC. During the conflict, Major Thapa,
officer commanding D Company, 1st
Battalion, 8th Gorkha Rifles, was taken
prisoner by the PLA when they overran
the undermanned Indian Army post
Srijap 1, Pangong Lake, Ladakh, on
20 October 1962. Thapa was awarded
the Param Vir Chakra (PVC) for his "cool
courage, conspicuous fighting qualities
and leadership . . . in the highest tradi-
tions of our Army".

Jaswant Garh War Monument, Nuranang, Arunachal Pradesh (former NEFA), to Rifleman Jaswant Singh Rawat, 4th Battalion, Garhwal Rifles, killed in action 17 November 1962. Rawat single-handedly defended an Indian Army post for three days. Only after shooting and killing him, did the PLA assailants discover that the Indian soldier had been on his own. In anger, the Chinese troops beheaded Rawat's body and took their trophy back to China. The head was returned by the Chinese after the ceasefire, together with a brass bust of the feted Indian rifleman. Rawat was posthumously awarded the Maha Vir Chakra (MVC), India's second-highest military decoration. The 4th Battalion, Garhwal Rifles, was bestowed with the Battle Honour 'Nuranang', the only one awarded in the Sino-Indian War of 1962.

6. LINE OF ACTUAL CONTROL

Just before midnight on 20 November, Beijing gave notice of its intention to cease hostilities in twenty-four hours. The declaration added that, with effect from 1 December 1962, its forces would withdraw to positions twenty kilometres behind the line of actual control which existed between China and India on 7 November 1959. It was expected that Indian forces also retired twenty kilometres from the line of actual control.

A week after China's unilateral ceasefire, in a missive to Nehru, Zhou Enlai stated that their proposed creation of a forty-kilometre demilitarized zone gave "full consideration to the decency, dignity and self-respect of both sides": neither country would face a gain or loss of territory. Zhou warned, however, that the ceasefire would not stop Chinese forces from retaliating should India not comply with the provisions of the truce. Nehru responded by charging that the Chinese had sparked the conflict by invading Indian territory to attack Indian Army posts. A frustrated Beijing then sent a terse note to New Delhi on 8 December, accusing the Indians of "deliberate haggling and evading an answer". The Chinese wanted to know whether the Indians agreed to the ceasefire. Did they agree to the demilitarized zone? Did they agree to the resuscitation of bilateral talks? But for Nehru and his government, there would be no bowing to Beijing's demands. The right to fight for legitimate Indian territory remained paramount, but not through negotiation. However, in spite of the political rhetoric, the Indian Army was ordered to observe the ceasefire and to stay back from the McMahon Line.

The reality on the NEFA battlefield, however, was that formal hostilities had ended with the demise of 48 Brigade and the fall of Chaku. In the western sector, the ceasefire was clear cut. After overwhelming the Indian posts at Rezing La within the Chinese claim line, the PLA did not try to take Chushul as the village did not fall within Chinese-claimed territory.

In NEFA, IV Corps was instructed to exercise maximum restraint when troops were on patrol, and to avoid any form of provocation or confrontation with any Chinese troops they encountered. Survivors of the Se La–Bomdi La sector battles continued to trickle onto the plains, but many perished from cold and hunger in their attempts to escape.

It would be three years before the Indian defence ministry placed casualty figures from all frontier operations against the Chinese in the public domain. Ninety per cent of casualties occurred in NEFA: 1,383 killed, 1,696 missing and 3,968 taken prisoner.

Tensions continuing, the Indian soldier is now armed with an SLR automatic rifle.

Similar casualty figures suffered by Chinese forces could only be estimated by the Indians. Where Indian troops displayed true mettle by receiving PLA attacks head on, Chinese troop casualties were significant. A good example of this was Thembang on 17 November when 5 Guards stood their ground, accounting for an estimated 300–400 Chinese killed. Also at Walong and Rezang La, returning Indian troops discovered ample evidence that the PLA had sustained significant casualties. The Indians did not take a single Chinese soldier prisoner.

In the aftermath of the conflict, during which much finger-pointing and apportioning of blame took place, the Indian Army command structure witnessed numerous changes.

On his return to New Delhi from Tezpur late on 19 November, Thapar resigned as Army Chief of Staff, to be replaced by General Jayanto Nath Chaudhuri OBE.

Kaul was relieved of his command of IV Corps and succeeded by General Sam Manekshaw, whose first order was to return corps HQ to Tezpur. Kaul was offered a transfer to command a training depot in the Punjab but he declined the offer and elected to resign instead.

General Sen retained his position as General Officer Commanding-in-Chief of Eastern Command until his resignation from the army several years later.

General Prasad, who had been relieved of his command of 4th Division, was reinstated after he had made a personal appeal to the Indian president. He was given another division in Western Command.

General A. S. Pathania, commander of the 4th Division during the fighting in the Se La–Bomdi sector resigned shortly after the Chinese declared the ceasefire.

Brigadier Dalvi remained a prisoner of war until May 1963 when he was released by the Chinese.

True to their assurances, on 1 December the Chinese commenced a systematic withdrawal, albeit at a slow pace. On the 5th, wounded Indian POWs were handed over at Bomdi La, but it would be another week before the PLA relinquished their occupation of the Indian garrison. In an unprecedented and somewhat bizarre gesture, the Chinese, while occupying Bomdi La, cleaned, stacked or parked the matériel left behind by the retreating Indians: small arms, mortars, artillery, vehicles, shells, ammunition, clothing and several American automatic rifles. The Chinese drew up a meticulous inventory for the Indians to sign upon collection. Whilst Beijing refused to make any political mileage out of the transaction, New Delhi accused the Chinese of adding humiliation to the Indians' defeat, and that Beijing was exploiting the event purely for propaganda purposes.

Since the clash of arms in 1962, further incidents have occurred between Chinese and Indian forces along the border. For five days in September 1967, the PLA attacked Indian posts at Nathu La, a mountain pass linking the Indian state of Sikkim with Tibet.

The following month, four miles northwest of Nathu La, there was a day-long scuffle between the two opposing forces at Cho La. Casualty figures from the two

The Nathu La border from India looking toward Bhutan. (Photo Thebrowniris)

incidents vary, with the Indians claiming 340 Chinese killed and 450 wounded, compared to Indian losses of 88 killed and 163 wounded.

In the latter half of 1971, India entered into to a peace, friendship and cooperation treaty with the Soviet Union, while China sided with Pakistan in its war with India.

In 1980, Indian Prime Minister Indira Gandhi endorsed a plan to upgrade troop levels along the Line of Actual Control and the infrastructural enhancement of disputed zones.

The next flashpoint arose during the winter of 1986. For two years, Indian troops had been actively patrolling the Sumdorong Chu valley just west of Tawang in the state of Arunachal Pradesh (NEFA until February 1987). PLA troops entered the valley in 1986 with a construction team to build a helicopter pad at Wandung. India's Chief of Army Staff at the time, General K. Sundarji, responded by airlifting a brigade to the region. By mid-1987, both sides backed down. The following year, Prime Minister Rajiv Gandhi visited Beijing, heralding a significant warming in relations between the two nations. Bilateral agreements in the fields of science, technology and culture resulted.

The early 1990s witnessed a further relaxation of military tension along the mutual frontiers as both sides agreed to cross-border liaison by the respective forces stationed along the borders. In 1993 and 1996, Sino-Indian bilateral peace and tranquillity accords were signed by the two nations, based on a desire to maintain peace along the Line of Actual Control. However, ten meetings of the Sino-Indian Joint Working Group (SIJWG) failed to reach a consensus to resolve the decades-old border question.

Indian nuclear tests led to a cooling of relations in 1998, particularly after Defence Minister George Fernandes's statement that "in my perception of national security, China is enemy No. 1 ... and any person who is concerned about India's security must agree with that fact". China remained opposed to India's entry into the nuclear club.

In 2006, in spite of the re-opening of the Nathu La Pass in Sikkim for trading, in November that year there was an acrimonious exchange of words between Beijing and New Delhi: China claimed ownership of the whole of Arunachal Pradesh (formerly NEFA), while the Indians alleged that the Chinese were occupying 24,000 square miles of Indian territory in Kashmir.

In October 2008, Britain changed its position on Tibet: "Tibet is part of China. Full stop."

A year later, the Asian Development Bank officially acknowledged Arunachal Pradesh as part of India, a decision that provoked Beijing's ire.

Economic cooperation and trade between the nations escalated in the 2010s, and in April 2011 at the BRICS (acronym for an association of five major emerging national economies: Brazil, Russia, India, China and South Africa) summit in Sanya, Hainan, China, the two countries agreed to restore defence cooperation across shared borders.

The cordial tone expressed by China and India would be strengthened further at the next BRICS summit in New Delhi in 2012.

In April/May 2013, a three-week standoff between Indian and PLA troops along the Actual Line of Control between Jammu and Kashmir's Ladakh region and Aksai Chin threatened to undo the reconciliatory efforts undertaken by both sides since the turn of the century. However, on 5 May the situation was amicably resolved as China agreed to withdraw its troops while India reciprocated with the removal of 'live-in' bunkers in the disputed Chumar zone.

As recently as 16 June–28 August 2017, there was another armed incident arising out of construction vehicles and PLA troops moving southward on the Doklam plateau into Indian-claimed territory. Two days later, Indian troops and two bulldozers moved into Doklam to stop the Chinese from their road construction.

The inevitable exchange of claims and counterclaims started between Beijing and New Delhi, with each categorically declaring ownership of that piece of real estate. The Chinese sited the 1890 Convention in support of their claim.

A remote Indian military helipad, Jammu and Kashmir. (Photo Piyush Tripathi)

An Indian soldier on the Chinese border. (Photo shankars)

On 15 August, there were reports from Ladakh that several Indian and PLA troops had been wounded in a skirmish after the Chinese, allegedly inadvertently, crossed into Indian-claimed territory. Two weeks later, both sides withdrew, thereby averting a dangerous situation from disintegrating into a full-scale battle. On 9 October, Beijing declared that it was ready to maintain peace on its borders with India.

Today, China is India's largest trading partner, while a fluctuating armed truce remains in place.

Index

Acknowledgements

My sincere thanks, as always, to Colonel Dudley Wall for his excellent drawings of maps and weapons. Thank you Chris Cocks, my commissioning editor, for his unfaltering support and belief in me.

These publications were helpful source material: Claude Arpi's *1962 and the McMahon Line Saga* (Lancer, Frankfort, 2013), *Asian Recorder*, declassified CIA reports, Lok Sabha parliamentary debates, Neville Maxwell's *India's China War* (Jonathan Cape, London, 1970), *Peking Review, People's Daily* (Beijing), *Statesman* (New Delhi) and *Times of India*.

About the Author

Born in Southern Rhodesia, now Zimbabwe, historian and author Gerry van Tonder came to Britain in 1999. Specializing in military history, Gerry has authored *Rhodesian Combined Forces Roll of Honour 1966–1981*; *Book of Remembrance: Rhodesia Native Regiment and Rhodesian African Rifles*; *North of the Red Line* (on the South African border war), and the co-authored definitive *Rhodesia Regiment 1899–1981*. Gerry presented a copy of the latter to the regiment's former colonel-in-chief, Her Majesty the Queen. Gerry writes extensively for several Pen & Sword military history series including 'Cold War 1945–1991', 'Military Legacy' (focusing on the heritage of British cities) and 'History of Terror'.

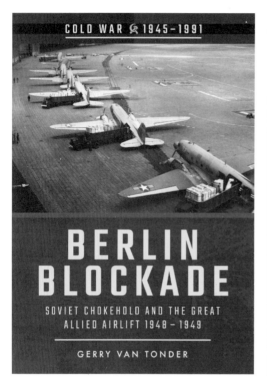

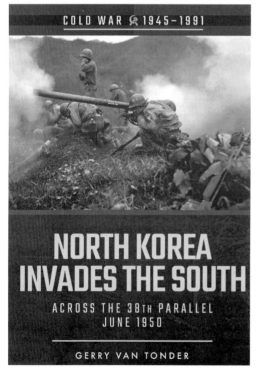
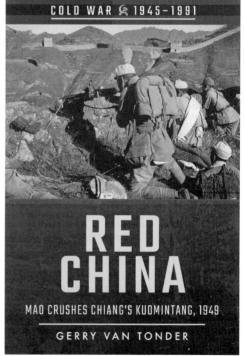